NIAMH CUSACK (Catherine)

Niamh previously a.......... .... in *Nabakov's Gloves*. Other **theatre** includes *Dancing At Lughnasa* (Old Vic); *Portrait of a Lady* (Theatre Royal, Bath); *Crestfall* (Theatre 503); *The Enchantment*, *His Dark Materials* (National Theatre); *The Way of the World* (Royal Theatre, Northampton); *Ghosts* (Gate, London); *Mammals*, *The Phoenix* (Bush Theatre); *Breathing Corpses* (Royal Court); *Indian Ink* (Aldwych); *The Merchant of Venice* (Chichester Festical Theatre); *The Three Sisters* (Gate, Dublin; Royal Court); *Playboy of the Western World* (West Yorkshire Playhouse); *The Admirable Crichton* (Triumph Productions/Haymarket); *Captain Swing* (Leeds Playhouse); *A Woman of No Importance*, *A Doll's House* (Gate, Dublin); *Learned Ladies*, *As You Like It*, *The Art of Success*, *Romeo and Juliet*, *Othello*, *Mary After the Queen* (Royal Shakespeare Company); *The Plough and the Stars* (Young Vic); *The Fairy Queen* (Aix en Provence); *The Tutor* (Old Vic); *The Three Sisters* (Manchester Royal Exchange); *The Maids* (Donmar Warehouse & Tour); *Not I* (Beckett Festival at The Barbican). **Films** include *Hereafter, 5 Minutes Of Heaven, The Closer You Get, Playboys*, Sh*adow Under The Sun, Paris By Night, Lucky Sunil, Fools Of Fortune*. **TV** includes *Lewis, Midsomer Murders, Fallen Angel, The Last Detective – Series 3, Miss Marple – 4.50 From Paddington, Too Good To Be True, State Of Mind, Trust, Little Bird, Always And Everyone, Rhinoceros, Colour Blind, Trauma, Heartbeat, Angel Train, Poirot, Jeeves and Wooster, Chalkface, A Marriage Of Inconvenience, Till We Meet Again*.

LISA KERR (Aggie)

Lisa graduated from LAMDA in 2008 and appeared in Out of Joint's recent *Mixed Up North*. **Theatre** credits include *The Old 100th* (Rehearsed reading of Conor Mitchell and Rachel O'Riordan's new writing, Theatre Royal, Drury Lane); *Election Idol* (Puddle Productions, Brighton Fringe Festival); *Peter Pan Kensington Gardens* (Script and Aerial Workshops with Ben Harrison, LAMDA/The Hangar); *The Musician* (Conor Mitchell's new Opera, Old Museum Arts Centre, Belfast); *The Sweetest Swing in Baseball* (LAMDA); *Cole Porter's 'Can-Can'* (LAMDA); *Prince of Tyre* (LAMDA); and *What The Butler Saw* (LAMDA). **Film** credits include *Re-Uniting the Rubins* and *Klink Klank Echoes*.

ALASTAIR MAVOR (Walter/Stefan)

Alastair's **theatre** includes *Scouts in Bondage* and *Boys of the Empire* (King's Head Theatre); Understudy for 'Taplow' in *The Browning Version* (Theatre Royal Bath & UK Tour); *The Best of Times* (reading dir. Andrew Hall); *What's Wrong With Angry* (Chandler Productions/Wild Justice); and *Someone Who'll Watch Over* (Hog Head, Edinburgh Fringe). **Short Films** include *Puny Earthlings* and *Youth*. **Radio** include *Boys of the Empire* for BBC Radio Scotland. Alastair is a member of the National Youth Theatre.

KATHRYN O'REILLY (Georgie)

Kathryn graduated from LAMDA in 2008 and appeared in Out of Joint's recent *Mixed Up North*. **Theatre** prior to training includes Jocasta in *Oedipus* directed by Marcello Magni and Raquel in *Don Juan* directed by Phil Willmott. **Television** and **film** credits include *The Bill*, *Rough Justice*, *Halal Harry* and *Zebra Crossings*.

DAVID RINTOUL (Dickens)

David spent eight years as a member of Joint Stock, appearing in *Fanshen*, *Speakers*, *Yesterday's News*, *Devil's Island*, *A Mad World My Masters*, *Epsom Downs* and *An Optimistic Thrust*. Other **theatre** includes *Myth, Propaganda & Disaster*, *Little Eyolf*, *Absolute Hell* (Orange Tree, Richmond); *Funny Girl* (Sheffield Crucible); *John Bull* (Bristol Old Vic); *Phaedre*, *Gaslight* (Royal Lyceum, Edinburgh); *The Beaux' Stratagem*, *Infidelities*, *The White Devil* (Lyric, Hammersmith); *Lady Windermere's Fan*, *The Winslow Boy*, *Sondheim's Putting It Together* (Chichester); *Sergeant Ola and his Followers*, *Etta Jenks* (Royal Court); *An Ideal Husband* (Old Vic); *Richard II*, *Richard III* (Phoenix); *As You Like It*, *A Mad World My Masters* (Shakespeare's Globe). On tour he has played Hamlet, Macbeth and Peer Gynt in the USA; Charles Surface in *School for Scandal* in India; Oberon in Malaysia and Indonesia; Malvolio in Egypt and Turkey. For the RSC: Henry IV 1&2, *Edward III*, *The Island Princess*, *Keepers of the Flame*, *The American Pilot*, *Breakfast With Mugabe*; for the National Theatre:

The World Turned Upside Down, *The Trojan War Will Not Take Place*, *A Midsummer Night's Dream*, *The Rivals* and *Remembrance of Things Past*. He has recently spent two years as Jake Houseman in the original London cast of *Dirty Dancing*. **Television** includes *Midsomer Murders*, *Sweet Medicine*, *Taggart*, *Poirot*, *Hornblower*, *Henry VIII*, *Lillie*, *The Mallens*, *The Cherry Orchard*, Mr Darcy in *Pride And Prejudice* and four series as ITV's *Doctor Finlay*. **Films** include *The Legend Of The Werewolf*, *Unrelated*, *Is Anybody There* and Polanski's *The Ghost*. David has also worked extensively on radio, voiced many documentaries and cartoons, and has recorded around 150 audio books.

DANNY SAPANI (Andersen)

Danny played the title role in Out of Joint's *Macbeth*, and appeared in *The Overwhelming* (National Theatre in association with Out of Joint). Other **theatre** includes *Wig Out*, *Neverland* (Royal Court); *Radio Golf* (Tricycle); *Big White Fog* (Almeida); *His Dark Materials*, *Antony and Cleopatra*, *The Machine Wreckers*, *Richard II* (National Theatre); *To the Green Fields Beyond* (Donmar Warehouse); *Julius Caesar* (Shakespeare's Globe); *The Silver Lake* (Wilton's Music Hall); *Measure for Measure* (Nottingham Playhouse); *Julius Caeser* (Royal Exchange, Manchester); *Measure for Measure* (Cheek by Jowl); *The Lion* (Talawa); *Love at a Loss* (Wild Iris); *The Beggars New Clothes* (Cockpit Theatre); *The Honest Whore* (Boulevard Theatre). **TV** includes *Misfits*, *Wild at Heart*, *Place of Execution*, *The Bill*, *Holby Blue*, *Blue Murder*, *Little Britain*, *Holby* City - Africa Special, *Serious and Organised*, *In Deep*, *Ultimate Force* Series I and II, *Holby City*, *Fish*, *Trial and Retribution*, *Shakespeare Shorts*, *Casualty*, *Richard II*, *Stick With Me Kid*, *Between The Lines*, *B&B*. **Films** include *The Oxford Murders*, *Song for a Raggy Boy*, *Anansi*, *Timecode II*, *Going Down The Road*.

LORNA STUART (Kate/Ellen)

Lorna graduated from LAMDA in 2008 and appeared in Out of Joint's recent *Mixed Up North* as Tamsin. **Theatre** credits include Susan in *The Lion, the Witch and the Wardrobe* (Antic Disposition) and Beakie in *Honk!* (Hotbox). Theatre whist training include Grusha in *The Caucasian Chalk Circle*, Thaisa in *Pericles*, Eve in *Can Can* and Varya in *The Cherry Orchard*. Television credits include Jen in *AAA* (Endemol). **Voice Overs** include *Poetry of Abandonment*.

SEBASTIAN BARRY Writer

Sebastian Barry was born in Dublin in 1955. His plays include *Boss Grady's Boys* (1988), *The Steward of Christendom* (1995), *Our Lady of Sligo* (1998), *The Pride of Parnell Street* (2007) and *Tales of Ballycumber* (2009). His novels include *The Whereabouts of Eneas McNulty* (1998), *Annie Dunne* (2002), *A Long Long Way* (2005) and *The Secret Scripture* (2008). He has won, among other awards, the Irish-America Fund Literary Award, the Christopher Ewart-Biggs Prize, the London Critics Circle Award and the Kerry Group Irish Fiction Prize. *A Long Long Way*, which was also shortlisted for the Man Booker Prize and the Dublin International Impac Prize, was the *Dublin: One City One Book* choice for 2007. *The Secret Scripture* won the Costa Book of the Year award, the Irish Book Awards for Best Novel and the Independent Booksellers Prize. It was shortlisted for the Man Booker Prize, Kerry Group Irish Fiction Award, Christopher Ewart-Biggs award and the James Tait Black Memorial Prize. He lives in Wicklow with his wife and three children.

TIM BRAY Lighting Designer

Tim recently lit Mixed Up North for Out of Joint and Bolton Octagon. Tim's Lighting Design credits include *The Rivals*, *The Rover, Iphigenia* (Southwark Playhouse); *Sisters Such Devoted Sisters* (Drill Hall), *Macbeth* (The Albany, Deptford); *Machinal* (BAC); *Out Of The Blue* (Nottingham Playhouse); *One Day In October* (Riverside Studios); *Sara* (The Bridewell); and *Jamais Vu* (Ken Cambell). Tim has toured extensively re-lighting various productions including: *Sweeney Todd* (RNT); *Anna Karenina* (Shared Experience); *Oliver Twist* (Lyric Hammersmith); *A Midsummer Night's Dream* (Tim Supple); *Convict's Opera, The Overwhelming* (National Theatre/Out of Joint): *O Go My Man* (Out of Joint/Royal Court), *Top Girls* (Oxford Stage Company); *The 39 Steps* (Fiery Angel); *The Glass Menagerie* (Theatre Royal Bath); *The Dumb Waiter* (Oxford Playhouse); *Highland Fling* (Matthew Bourne) and *Fat Pig* (Comedy Theatre).

GRAHAM COWLEY Producer

Out of Joint's Producer since 1998. His long collaboration with Max Stafford-Clark began as Joint Stock Theatre Group's first General Manager for seven years in the 1970s. He was General Manager of the Royal Court for eight years, and on their behalf transferred a string of hit plays to the West End. His career has spanned the full range of theatre production, from small fringe companies to major West End shows and large scale commercial tours. Outside Out of Joint, he has translated Véronique Olmi's *End of Story* (Chelsea Theatre) and has produced the 'Forgotten Voices from the Great War' series of plays including *What the Women Did* (Southwark Playhouse, 2004), *Red Night* by James Lansdale Hodson (Finborough, 2005) and *My Real War 1914-?*, based on the letters of a young WW1 soldier, which toured twice in 2007 and played at Trafalgar Studios in October 2009. The final play in the series, *The Searcher* by Velona Pilcher, is due to appear in 2010.

CAROLYN DOWNING Sound Designer

Carolyn designed the sound for *Flight Path* (Out of Joint/Bush Theatre); other sound designs include: *Krieg Der Bilder* (Staatsheater Mainz, Germany); After *Dido* (English National Opera at Young Vic); *Dimetos, Absurdia* (Donmar Warehouse); *All My Sons* (Schoenfeld Theatre, New York); *Tre Kroner-Gustav III* (Royal Dramatic Theatre, Sweden); *Angels in America* (Headlong Theatre); *The Winter's Tale, Pericles, Days of Significance* (Royal Shakespeare Company);*The Kreutzer Sonata, Vanya, State Of Emergency, The Internationalist* (Gate); *Oxford Street, Alaska* (Royal Court); *Ghosts, Dirty Butterfly* (Young Vic); *After Miss Julie, Othello* (Salisbury Playhouse); *Moonlight & Magnolias* (Tricycle Theatre); *Topdog / Underdog* (Sheffield Crucible Studio); *A Whistle In The Dark, Moonshed* (Royal Exchange Theatre, Manchester); If That's All There Is, *Hysteria* (Inspector Sands); *Arsenic and Old Lace* (Derby Playhouse); *The Water Engine* (Theatre 503, in association with The Young Vic); *Blood Wedding* (Almeida); *Gone To Earth* (Shared Experience); *Waiting For The Parade* (Mountview Academy of Theatre Arts); *No Way Out* (Huis Clos), *Stallerhof, A Doll's House, The Double Bass, The Provoked Wife* and *Mongoose* (Southwark Playhouse); *The Watery Part of the World* (Sound and Fury). Carolyn's associate sound design credits include: *Some Trace of Her, Fix Up* (National Theatre)*; The Overwhelming* (National Theatre in association with Out of Joint); *O Go My Man, Macbeth; Forty Winks* (Royal Court) and *By The Bog Of Cats* (Wyndhams). Other credits include Assistant to the Sound Designer on *Billy Elliot: The Musical* and No.1 sound operator on *Blood Brothers* at the Phoenix Theatre.

MIKA HANDLEY Assistant Designer

Mika trained at Motley Theatre Design Course and Royal Scottish Academy of Music and Drama. Recent Design credits include: *The Long Way Home* (Eastern Angles, Tour), *The Rover* (Southwark Playhouse), *Return to Akenfield* (Eastern Angles, Tour),*50 Ways To Leave Your Lover at Christmas* (Bush Theatre), *The Recurring Rise and Fall* (Michael Frayn Space, Hampstead Theatre), *50 Ways to Leave Your Lover* tour (Bush Theatre, Norwich Playhouse, Oxford North Wall, Latitude Festival), *Comp* (Tristan Bates Theatre), *Heritage* (New Athenaeum Theatre, Glasgow), Associate Artist for *Present:Tense 12* (Nabokov) Assistant Designer credits include: *The Brothers Size* (Young Vic/ATC), *Don Carlo* (Royal Opera House), *The Final Shot* (Theatre 503). Mika was a finalist for the Linbury Prize for Stage Design 2007, and won the Royal Opera House Award. In 2008, a JMK Directors Award proposal won the Ian Ritchie Foundation Award.

JULIAN LITTMAN Musical Director

Julian recently worked on *Dreams of Violence* (Out of Joint/Soho). Other **recent theatre** includes MD for *Hot Mikado*, *The Mummy's Tomb*, *Up On The Roof*, *Twelfth Night*; and appearances in *The Comedy Of Errors* (also MD), *Sweeny Todd*, *A Funny Thing Happened On The Way To The Forum* and *The Gambler* (all Queen's Theatre, Hornchurch). MD for *Cinderella* (New Wolsey Theatre, Ipswich); *Vanity Fair* (Chicken Shed Theatre Company); *Laurel And Hardy* (New Vic, Stoke); *Time's Up* (Yvonne Arnaud Theatre, Guildford); *Kafka's Dick* (Salisbury Playhouse); *Pump Boys And Dinettes* (also MD) (Haymarket, Basingstoke). West End Theatre includes *We Will Rock You*, *Jailhouse Rock*, *125th Street*, *Budgie*, *Hedwig & The Angry Inch*, *Pump Boys And Dinettes*, *Pilgrim*, *Fire Angel*, and *Return To The Forbidden Planet*. **Television** includes *Holby City*, *Doctors*, *The Bill*, *Crocodile Shoes*, *Juliet Bravo*, *The Sweeney*, *Baal*, *The Lenny Henry Show*, *Hammer House Of Horror*, *Not The Nine O'Clock News* and countless plays. **Films** include *Running Scared*, *The Life And Death Of Peter Sellers*, *Al's Lads*, *Mad About Mambo*, *Evita*, *Dancing Thru The Dark* and *The American Way*. Julian has written **songs** for Sheena Easton, Sister Sledge, Charlie Dore, Toto Coelo and Philip Bailey. He has played with Gerry Rafferty, Dexy's Midnight Runners, Pete Townshend, and his music has been featured in *Playing For Keeps* (Miramax Pictures) and *Lukas & Protocol* starring Goldie Hawn. He recently co-produced and arranged the upcoming Charlie Dore album *The Hula Valley Songbook*.

THOMAS MOORE Songs

Moore was born in Dublin in 1779. Like Sebastian Barry and Max Stafford-Clark he was educated at Trinity College; he then studied Law in London. He found fame as a poet, translator, balladeer and singer, with his ballads published as Moore's Irish Melodies in 1846 and 1852. Moore was a successful society figure in London. In 1803 he was appointed registrar to the Admiralty in Bermuda. From there, he travelled in Canada and the United States (travels which inspired his writing). He returned to England and married an actress, Elizabeth "Bessy" Dyke, in 1811. Financial troubles forced Moore to leave Britain for Paris in 1819 where he spent time with Lord Byron. He became Byron's literary executor and was much criticised later for allowing himself to be persuaded to destroy Byron's memoirs at the behest of Byron's family. Moore finally settled in Wiltshire, and became a novelist and biographer as well as a successful poet. All of his five children died within his lifetime. He died in 1852.

LUCY OSBORNE Set and Costume Designer

Lucy designed *Dreams of Violence* for Out of Joint and Soho Theatre. Other recent theatre credits include *Twelfth Night* for the Chicago Shakespeare Theater (winner of the Jefferson Award for Scenic Design, nominated for Costume Design); *Shades* for the Royal Court's Young Writers Festival; *Macbeth* (Edinburgh Lyceum/Nottingham Playhouse) and *Wrecks*, Broken

Space Festival, *2,000 Feet Away*, *Tinderbox* and *tHe dYsFUnCKshOnalZ!* (all for the Bush Theatre, for whom she is an Associate Artist). She designed *Artefacts* (Nabakov Theatre Company / Bush) and *Some Kind of Bliss* (Trafalgar Studios), both of which transferred to the 2008 'Brits off Broadway Festival' in New York and other theatre credits include *Be My Baby* (New Vic Theatre); *Rope* (Watermill Theatre); *Closer* (Theatre Royal Northampton); *The Long and the Short and the Tall* (Sheffield Lyceum); *The Prayer Room* (Birmingham Rep/Edinburgh Festival); *Ship of Fools* (set, Theatre 503); *The Unthinkable* (Sheffield Crucible Studio) and *Season of Migration to the North* (RSC New Writing Season). Future work includes *Taming of the Shrew* (Chicago Shakespeare Theater) and *The Whisky Taster* (Bush Theatre). Lucy graduated from Motley Theatre Design School, having also gained a BA in Fine Art from the University of Newcastle.

MAX STAFFORD-CLARK Director

Educated at Trinity College, Dublin, Max Stafford-Clark co-founded Joint Stock Theatre Group in 1974 following his Artistic Directorship of The Traverse Theatre, Edinburgh. From 1979 to 1993 he was Artistic Director of The Royal Court Theatre. In 1993 he founded the touring company, Out of Joint. His work as a Director has overwhelmingly been with new writing, and he has commissioned and directed first productions by many leading writers, including Sue Townsend, Stephen Jeffreys, Timberlake Wertenbaker, Sebastian Barry, April de Angelis, Mark Ravenhill, Andrea Dunbar, Robin Soans, Alistair Beaton, Stella Feehily, David Hare and Caryl Churchill. In addition he has directed classic texts including *The Seagull*, *The Recruiting Officer* and *King Lear* for the Royal Court; *A Jovial Crew*, *The Wives' Excuse* and *The Country Wife* for The Royal Shakespeare Company; and *The Man of Mode*, *She Stoops to Conquer*, *Three Sisters* and *Macbeth* for Out of Joint. He directed David Hare's *The Breath of Life* for Sydney Theatre Company in 2003. Academic credits include an honorary doctorate from Oxford Brookes University and Visiting Professorships at the Universities of Hertfordshire, Warwick and York. His books are *Letters to George* and *Taking Stock*.

JESSICA SWALE Associate Director

This is Jessica's fourth production with Out of Joint, for whom she is resident Associate Director. She is Artistic Director of Red Handed Theatre Company, for whom recent credits include *The Rivals* (Southwark Playhouse), *Mad Kings and Englishmen, The School for Scandal, A Midsummer Night's Dream, Twelfth Night* (Bridewell Theatre), *The Glass Tower* (Pleasance Theatre); for 'a single leaf', *Finding Alice* (National tour) and choreography for the Unicorn Theatre, the Union and The American Globe, New York. Jessica will be directing *Macbeth* in Yunnan, China in 2010 for Youth Bridge Global, an International NGO which uses theatre as a development tool, having enjoyed directing *A Comedy of Errors* in the Marshall Islands (2008) and *Much Ado about Nothing* in Bosnia in Herzegovina (2009).

"You expect something special from Out of Joint"
The Times

Out of Joint is a national and international touring
theatre company dedicated to the development
and production of new writing. Under the direction
of Max Stafford-Clark the company has premiered
plays from leading writers including David Hare,
Caryl Churchill, David Edgar, Alistair Beaton, Sebastian Barry,
Robin Soans and Timberlake Wertenbaker, as well as introducing
first-time writers such as Simon Bennett, Stella Feehily, Mark
Ravenhill and David Watson.

"Max Stafford-Clark's excellent Out of Joint company"
The Independent

Touring all over the UK, Out of Joint frequently performs at and
co-produces with key venues such as the Royal Court and the
National Theatre and recently with Sydney Theatre Company.
The company has performed in six continents. Back home,
Out of Joint also pursues an extensive education programme.

"Out of Joint is out of this world"
Boston Globe

In autumn 2010, Out of Joint will present the world premiere
of *The Big Fellah* by Richard Bean, set across three decades,
among IRA supporters in New York.

Shopping and Fucking
by Mark Ravenhill (2006).
Photo: John Haynes

Mixed Up North by Robin Soans
(2009). Photo: Ian Tilton

A complete list of our previous productions is available on www.outofjoint.co.uk

Keep in touch

For information on our shows, tour details and offers, get in touch (contact details below) letting us know whether you'd like to receive information by post or email. Find us on Facebook, and follow us on Twitter too!

Bookshop

Scripts of many of our previous shows are available at exclusive discounted prices from our online shop:
www.outofjoint.co.uk

Education

Out of Joint offers a diverse programme of workshops and discussions for groups coming to see our performances. For full details of our education programme, resource packs or *Our Country's Good* workshops, contact Panda at Out of Joint.

HampsteadTheatre

Hampstead Theatre is one of the UK's leading new writing companies – a company that has just celebrated its fiftieth year of operation.

Throughout its long history the theatre has existed to support a thriving local, national and international playwriting culture. We commission plays in order to enrich and enliven this culture. We support, develop and produce the work of new writers, emerging writers, established writers, mid-career writers and senior writers and have a proud tradition for creating the conditions for their plays and careers to develop.

The list of playwrights who had their early work produced at Hampstead Theatre and who are now filling theatres all over the country and beyond include Mike Leigh, Michael Frayn, Brian Friel, Terry Johnson, Hanif Kureishi, Simon Block, Abi Morgan, Rona Munro, Tamsin Oglesby, Harold Pinter, Shelagh Stephenson, debbie tucker green, Crispin Whittell, Roy Williams and Dennis Kelly.

The Creative Learning programme is also an integral part of Hampstead Theatre's work. We aim to celebrate all aspects of the creative process in ways which support learning and widen access to the theatre's programme. Inspiring creativity and developing emerging talent, at its best our work has the power to change lives.

In recent years we have been proud to establish a strong tradition of collaborating with some of the country's leading repertory and touring theatre companies, including two previous productions with Out of Joint. We are delighted to be working together once again on *Andersen's English*.

Hampstead Theatre, Eton Avenue, Swiss Cottage, London NW3 3EU
www.hampsteadtheatre.com
Registered Charity number: 218506

Hampstead Theatre Staff

Sebastian Barry
Andersen's English

ff

faber and faber

First published in 2010
by Faber and Faber Limited
74–77 Great Russell Street
London WC1B 3DA

Typeset by Country Setting, Kingsdown, Kent CT14 8ES
Printed in England by CPI Bookmarque, Croydon, Surrey

A CIP record for this book
is available from the British Library

To Dinah Wood

Characters

Andersen
the writer, fifty-two and sixty-five

Dickens
the writer, forty-six

Catherine
his wife, plump, pretty, exhausted, forty-two

Walter
his second eldest son, sixteen

Kate
his daughter, nineteen

Georgie
Catherine's younger sister, thirty

Aggie
a maid, Irish, sixteen

Ellen
an Irish actress, eighteen

Stefan
a young Danish friend of Andersen's, eighteen

The part of Ellen is doubled by Kate,
the part of Stefan by Walter

ANDERSEN'S ENGLISH

Act One

Downstage, Andersen sits reading a newspaper in the company of his young friend Stefan. It is part of Andersen's room in Copenhagen, on the day of or after Charles Dickens' death, June 1870.
Upstage in shadow are other figures in stillness, like a painting in a dark church.

Andersen (*a newspaper*) Poor Dickens dead, my dear Stefan. Most extraordinary, most sad. It brings back so many memories of my days with him in England. Long long ago, it seems, like in an old story, but it is only a dozen years ago.

Stefan To think of so great a man extinguished, gone from the earth.

Andersen It scarcely seems the same world, suddenly, without his presence in it. I had such great love for him, such reverence. I am shocked in my very soul to consider that he, a younger man, leaves the earth before me. Twelve years ago he was in the highest vigour of life. I myself felt tired and old already. My health was poor. My spirits were heavy. He treated me with the loving courtesy due an older brother. It is true that, though I wrote to him many times over the years, for some reason he never replied. But while I lived with him his care, his perspicuity were extraordinary, though his establishment was humble enough. There was a little maid, I remember, that showed me kindness. (*Claps his hands.*) I wonder what became of her? Of them all? Because of course, my dear Stefan, not long after I left them, the great cataclysm, the great revolution in Dickens' life occurred.

Stefan Such a *bouleversement* had rarely been seen in the world of literature. You were aware of it while you stayed among them?

Andersen It seemed like a paradise of human hearts. I suppose I was dimly aware of mysteries. But I did not suspect trouble so great, no, no. I wrote about my stay among them shortly after, and it seemed natural to describe them as happy. For, Stefan, their world there was sublime.

Stefan (*stroking Andersen's face*) I have read those beautiful pages.

Andersen Now as I look back, I understand it better.

Stefan You did sense it, you sensed it, Andersen – with your accustomed and admirable sensitivity.

Andersen I sensed not enough. Such it is to have no language. So are the passions of intimates hidden from the stranger. Now all that world is taken away, Dickens and his wife Catherine, waiting for me in that enchanted house he named Gad's Hill, as I toiled up from the little country station, burdened by my cases and, as ever, as ever, by my melancholy heart . . .

Stefan Dear Andersen.

Andersen And, and, dear Stefan, by my highly regrettable lack of English. Andersen's English, my dear friend, a horror and a hindrance.

This fading, and the sound of a young woman singing a Thomas Moore song. It's Kate, Dickens' daughter; as she sings 'Believe Me, if All Your Endearing Young Charms' the scene gathers round her.

A provisional Victorian 'room' in Gad's Hill Place, June 1857.

*The garden suggested, a landscape of rooms and the
real landscape, the distant sea, the snaking Thames,
the marshes between.
Catherine Dickens is reading.
Georgina Hogarth, Catherine's younger sister,
seated, is sewing a ribbon on a child's straw hat.
In the garden, Dickens is with his son Walter, sixteen.*

Dickens Do you feel you have any particular aptitude
whose existence I have neglected?

Walter No, Father.

Dickens There is no disgrace in that. In this age of wonders
you might do many things without any particular gift.

Walter But, India, Papa? A soldier? I do not know what
the heart of a soldier is. And every day in the newspaper
we read of horrors there.

Dickens It is a blessed matter to go out upon the world
as a young person. The highest good, the highest joy. To
start to make your way in your profession. To catch the
eye of some sweet, gentle girl. To begin, to begin. It is our
human bliss. This time never to come again. I cannot
provision my army of seven boys for ever, Walt. Think
of the others away at school in France. They come up
behind you like a tide.

Walter is weeping.

*The sound of the Thomas Moore song being played on
the piano somewhere in the house.
Kate sits at her easel.*

Catherine What are you doing, Georgie?

Georgie Plorn needs a hat for Sunday service.

*Dickens comes in, goes to the window and opens the
curtains wider.*

Dickens I think you will find it is traditional in England to open the curtains during the day. Was that you singing, Kate?

Catherine It was. And they are open, Charles.

Dickens We must have light, more light. I have written like a demon all day and now I am ready to be human again. (*Looking out.*) There is the porter from Higham station, carrying a box, a portmanteau and possibly a hatbox. And a most curious figure hobbling along behind him.

Catherine We are not expecting anyone.

Dickens (*looking at Georgie*) Putting black ribbons on hats is a deplorable pursuit.

Georgie rises and shepherds Dickens to his seat, watched by Catherine. Georgie puts a hand on Dickens' shoulder.

The horrors of the English funeral, mourners in black, horses in black, and hatbands in black.

Georgie smiling at him.

Georgie It is not for a funeral, Charles, only for little Plorn to go to chapel in.

Dickens That is a different matter.

Kate I am attempting a portrait of Plorn in his Sunday suit. I am aware, Papa, that not spilling paint on the floor is more important to you than any artistry I might possess.

Dickens (*turning about a little*) How are you, Catherine?

Catherine I am very well.

Dickens You say you are well, and I am glad that you say it.

Catherine looks at him.

That was beautiful singing, beautiful singing.

A little maid, Aggie, comes in.

Aggie Sir, there is a gentleman come.

Dickens What is his name, Aggie?

Aggie He doesn't know, sir.

Dickens Oh?

Aggie He's just all gobbledygook, sir. I asked him for a card but I might as well have asked him where Jonah was.

Kate Where is Jonah?

Aggie Why, in the whale, miss.

Kate Oh.

Dickens He doesn't know his own name by heart?

Aggie Seemingly not, sir. And then he was crying for a bit.

Dickens Why so?

Aggie Because I told him to go away, of course.

She hands Dickens some letters.
Andersen suddenly appears in the door.
He approaches Dickens.

Dickens A prowler, a poor vagabond? You seek something, sir? But no, no, I know this face. It is . . .

Andersen kisses him on the face.

Oh!

Andersen (*on the verge of tears*) You – has – I am – so – (*He openly weeps.*)

13

Dickens . . . Andersen, Hans Andersen . . .

Andersen Train surging on road of iron – all this way my – stomach . . . (*Describes eruption with his arms.*) Vesuvius. I struggle, I sweat, but heart leap, I am in land of Dicken . . .

Catherine Dear Andersen, you are most welcome. You have appeared, like an angel.

Andersen stares.

Dickens Andersen, we are most profoundly glad to see you. I have the warmest of memories of your visit at Broadstairs. Do you remember? It was your last day in England, and you sat with us at our simple table, when all the children were small, and some did not even exist. This is my girl, Kate – you remember her, Andersen?

Andersen Ah, ah.

Dickens And I said to you, come and see us again at the earliest opportunity, and Andersen, you come, to our new house – ten years later. By my eyes.

Georgie He may have the nice room on the second landing, Aggie.

Catherine Let me do that work of directing where he will sleep.

Georgie Well, shall he go to another room, Catherine?

Catherine He may do well where you bid him go.

Dickens Yes. You will have a view of the old marshes, and the sea beyond, if the mist allows. And our River Thames. And there is a little graveyard there, I know, somewhere, because once as a little boy I stood there with my father. I have made this little world, but do not know entirely where it is.

Andersen (*fearful*) Graveyard?

Dickens You will go with Aggie here? Go with Aggie? Will you bring him?

Aggie Yes, sir.

Andersen Oh, I declare my friendship, for you, dear Dicken. Farewell.

Dickens Farewell.

Andersen goes out with Aggie.

He reminds me of no one except himself and that must be a good thing. Will you be able to assimilate him, Georgie?

Catherine is about to speak.

Georgie Oh, I will have to be able.

Dickens Noble Georgie. (*The letters.*) Ah, ah, I read here, Andersen is to come today. Well, that is not news now. And here, this is in Wilkie Collins' hand . . . (*Opening a letter, scanning it, slumping in a chair.*) Oh, dear, dear Lord.

Georgie What is it, Charles?

Dickens Oh, my dear, I find – Expected, of course, but – I – (*He wipes his forehead.*) Grief, palpable grief . . .

Georgie goes to him, Catherine watching.

My poor dear friend, Douglas Jerrold. He is dead, my dear.

Kate Oh, Papa, do not weep.

Light now on a guest room. Andersen is just outside the 'door', reading some framed writing. The voices below.

Andersen (*reading, in his bad accent*) 'But my lads, my lads, tomorrow morning by four o'clock early, at Gad's Hill, there are pilgrims going to Canterbury with rich offerings . . .' (*To himself.*) Noble Shakspeare . . . Noble Shakspeare . . .

He goes on into the room, smiling at first.

It is – cold . . .

Aggie (*entering with some of his bags*) There is no fire, sir, because you were not expected.

Andersen goes to the window to look out.

There's no water neither in your basin. Your – yes – (*looking*) your pot, sir, is under the bed. I have to bring in a flame from another room to light your candle, sir.

Andersen immediately goes to the 'bed'; he presses it for softness and is not convinced. Aggie dips back with her taper lit. She lights the candle with the taper. Soft light, and the softer light of the distant sea.

Andersen It is – hard. So cold, so cold.

Aggie I am sorry, sir. It is June, but it's more like March, sir, isn't it?

Andersen takes off his large-sized shoes and gratefully squeezes his feet.
He takes one of his bags and extracts a length of rope. He brings it to the window and leans out and lets down the rope.

What are you doing, sir?

Andersen If there is fire, girl, I climb down the rope.

Aggie That is unusual, sir.

Andersen Hermm?

Aggie To carry a rope for that purpose.

Andersen (*defensively*) It is also good for – horse.

Aggie You have a horse with you, sir?

Andersen No, no, I mean say – oh, English – wild horse.

Aggie Oh, of course, sir. You mean a runaway horse. Well, yes, a rope is a handy thing, sir – if you can catch it. But of course, that is the point of a runaway horse. You cannot.

Aggie feels a moment of faintness.

Oh.

Andersen What is matter?

Aggie I told cook I couldn't eat nothing for breakfast. But cook said – but you don't need to know what cook said, sir. Excusing me. (*She goes.*)

Andersen coils the rope again and lies on the bed with it.

Andersen (*in Danish*) Lord, give me good English to converse with beautiful Dickens, Amen.

A few moments pass, Andersen sleeping.

Light up on Dickens, dressed for dinner now, Georgie with him. He is reading the letter. While they speak, a table is being set for dinner beyond them, the candles lit etc.

Dickens Do you know, Georgie, I think he was one of the sweetest men that ever lived. Hard in his way, sardonical, because he was so brilliant, you know, but in his centre, sweet, oh, and endearing, infinitely. Poor Jerrold.

Georgie It is very sad.

Dickens Plorn will need the black ribbon for a funeral after all. One should be careful what one says. The gods are always listening.

Georgie They do seem attentive, yes.

Dickens Friend Wilkie says here that he is certain there will be no money left to Mrs Jerrold, and I tell you, we can do something about that. Why, I may do some readings, perhaps Thackeray will do likewise, I am sure he will, he is a man of good heart, I will write to him immediately – and myself and Kate, and Charlie and Walt, and Wilkie himself, might attempt again *The Frozen Deep*.

Georgie That is a certain, solid, money-making thing.

Adersen suddenly awakes, startled and unhappy, struggling with the rope, Aggie hurrying in.

Aggie What, sir?

Andersen (*very distressed*) Graveyard, graveyard. I am bury me alive.

Aggie No, no, sir. You're among the living still.

Andersen (*looking about, gripping her hand*) Where I am, child?

Aggie In England, sir, at Gad's Hill, at the house of Mr Dickens, sir.

Andersen Thank God, thank God.

Aggie Oh, yes, sir, thank God. So say all of us.

Dickens (*with Georgie again*) Of course he was not so old – a few mere years ahead of me . . . Fifty-four. In his prime. I will raise – two thousand pounds, that shall be my aim, and I will do it. Let there be grief certainly, let there be weeping, but also, doing, doing, Georgie. For there is no doubt, no doubt at all, he was a deep, deep friend, and I am made smaller, darker, stranger by his going.

Aggie (*with Andersen again*) You may put on your black shoes, sir. They do want you for dinner.

Andersen Hey, hey? Yes, yes, I come, I come.

Aggie Let me help you, sir. Now, now.

She slips on his shoes for him. Andersen is weeping.

Ah, why do you cry, sir? Here's a handkerchief. I would bet a half-crown you have much finer than that, but where is it when you need it?

Andersen takes it, checks it for dirt, uses it.

He joins the others. Catherine brings him to his place. By now the table is suggested by light, candles lit. The garden breathes its cooling flowers. In the distance, the bells of churches. The landscape touched by the weakening sun. Kate, and the 'figures' of Mamie, the eldest son Charlie Junior, little Plorn (worked by the actors) and Walt in reality, a thrum and hum of family, Andersen introduced to the siblings, nodding and talking. Dickens strides forward to the table, joins the babble. There is a music that seems to be made up of the voices, thrumming louder, the lights blazing brighter, as if the fact of family was swallowing everything, grief, time, real things. Then suddenly it quietens.

Dickens Dear Andersen – you are quite rested? Aggie has given you what you needed?

Andersen The bed was cold, dear Dickens, a little little.

Dickens Oh, I am terribly sorry if you were cold. I will remind Aggie to warm your bed tonight.

Catherine The bed was not warmed because of dear Mr Andersen's unexpected arrival.

Dickens We must see ahead in matters of the household. We must peer into the future, and have water jars at the ready.

Catherine I am not quite sure why *I* am being upbraided about it. There is another to whom this task might be considered to have fallen. And who gets the praise when things go well.

Dickens Am I not correct in this, Georgie? Sit up straight, Charlie. Kate – fork. (*Meaning to correct how she is holding it.*)

Kate Father, I am nineteen. If I cannot hold my fork correctly by now, it is too late.

Dickens You will thank me when you are dining with princes.

Kate (*humorously*) I will dine only with savages if ever I leave here. It will be a rule with me.

Andersen The view touch me. Loveliness of England. Of this Kent. Gold river under sun and one black ship, then I – dreaming – graveyard, wake in coffin, alive, and me – (*making gesture of scratching*) lid . . .

Dickens By my eyes.

Andersen My English.

Dickens I understand you perfectly. Your English is excellent.

Andersen So, so? I am beautiful, happy.

Dickens (*to Charlie*) All is well at the magazine, Charlie?

Charlie It is sometimes confusing work, Papa.

Dickens *Household Words*, Andersen, where things familial find their most ardent defenders, where the poetry of the hearth is set forth: a man, a woman and their offspring, gathered in a peaceful group in this eternal England. Charlie has just begun in this work and I have high hopes for his efficiency in it.

Catherine I am so proud of him, Mr Andersen. Such a good, diligent boy.

Dickens Kate of course is painting.

Kate (*humorously*) I-am-painting. That's Kate.

Catherine Charles, I am thinking.

Dickens (*a touch impatiently*) Yes?

Catherine Was it not just the other week you saw poor Douglas?

Dickens Indeed, yes.

Catherine And how was he then – I seem to remember you noticing he was unwell? I ask because of course he was my friend also.

Dickens Yes, Catherine. He was unwell that day. And all week I was receiving reports from his London friends. As of a ship sailing onto the rocks. We know not the time nor the place, eh, Andersen?

Andersen (*startled*) Excuse?

Dickens It is our little lot as humans. The penalty for the gift of life. I say it lightly but mean it seriously. Boys, girls, *carpe diem*, bathe to your ears in the sweet water of youth.

Georgie I am sure youth characterises you still, Charles.

Catherine I am sure, I am sure.

Dickens Well, I thank you. Vigour is still mine, thank God. And yet I will not exult in life when poor Douglas now has gone under the waves. It was the day, Catherine, that Russell was to read from his Crimean journal – do you know his writings, Andersen? He was a newspaperman for *The Times* at the Crimea, a wonderful man, an Irishman of distinction – well, we were going about together, and Jerrold was showing Russell how one should read to the public, because he had heard him on a previous occasion, and did not think Russell understood the secret, but was generously going to show him the secret, and every now and then Jerrold was complaining of some inward pain, in a very nice, unaffected manner. He said some fresh paint had been put on his study window the day before, and he suspected the fumes had poisoned him, and he felt seedy. But we went out to Greenwich together before the reading, and his spirits were waxing and waning, and the three of us walked up to the top of Shooter's Hill, and by heavens we marked out Inkerman on the ground – (*does so on the table*) where the Second Division lay in the scrub –

As he speaks Aggie is drawn more and more into the narrative.

– in this instance, these napkins, and the Russian land army coming along at them in the fog – that is to say, this great serving plate – and the great horde of troops out of Sebastopol itself, and the British and French armies ready together, and from six in the morning enduring the pounding of the Russian barrage, and then all violence and death till half past three, when at last the Russians were driven back, and five Victoria Crosses that day for the soldiers, by God . . . Irish soldiers, Aggie, because they always put the Irish in the front line. They are considered excellent soldiers for bearing the brunt of an attack.

Aggie Oh! Brave boys!

Georgie Thank you, Aggie.

Dickens Yes, Aggie, and by then as you may imagine, Jerrold was so excited, and jumping about, all vigour and life, as I was myself, and Russell laughing at us, and Jerrold declared he had quite got over the paint. And then he was all head back and laughing at some nonsense I was speaking, in our old manner, and we were as easy as chairs. But it was only the start of a week of enormous suffering for him. His fine white hair and his frail hands, that is what I remember. Wilkie says he was eloquent, brave and admirable to the last.

Georgie Oh, Charles.

Kate Poor Papa.

Walter They say there were two thousand of our soldiers killed that day, and twenty thousand Russians.

Charlie Huzza!

Dickens Yes, yes, Walt – and Russell himself the next morning, marvelling at the number of Russians lying there. How vividly he read that night, after Jerrold had set him straight. And Jerrold, Jerrold, *Black Ey'd Susan*, the most natural nautical English play since Shakespeare's *Tempest*. (*To Walt.*) When you are an old man, Walt, they will still be playing that in England.

Walter Am I to be an old man, Papa? I did not know.

Catherine puts a hand on his sleeve.

Catherine My dear.

Dickens Oh yes, Walt, I hope so.

Andersen (*nodding*) Ah, Shakspeare, noble Shakspeare . . .

Dickens And noble Jerrold. Noble, gentle Jerrold. Let us raise our glasses, my dears, to a delicate, happy and much-missed man.

They raise their glasses and drink. Andersen thinks he is being drunk to, and rises.

Andersen Thank you, dear, dear Dickens – it is – mountain – high, high love – that feel me . . . And to your back I say – *skaal!* – long life.

Walter He was not drinking to . . .

Dickens Long life indeed. (*Sternly looking at Walt.*) Walter, as you are going out to India in a few days, you must learn discretion.

Catherine Charles, do not say so lightly that he is going. To that terrifying place. No, no, forgive me. (*A moment.*) Charles, maybe Mr Andersen while he is here would like to see the Crystal Palace? I am going there myself next week, and might find him a ticket if he wished – they are to give *The Messiah*, with a choir of two thousand souls.

Dickens Well, that is an awful lot of singing. I am afraid I will be much in town now myself, if I am to make arrangements for Jerrold's family. At least there are only five children. It was my fate to have so great a crowd of them, Andersen, that I meet them in the corridors in the night, and think I have prowlers. One night I may shoot one.

Mamie Papa . . .

Catherine I hope you would not kill one of our children.

Dickens Of course not, madam – since it was you made them in the first place. It's just that you made so many.

Kate (*quite sternly*) You would be quite lost without us, Papa.

Catherine And I would be married then to a murderer, and I would not like that.

Dickens (*a moment*) Andersen, cricket? You look like a bowler. Look – like – a – bowler.

Andersen (*puzzling the words*) Bowler?

Dickens does the action of the bowler.

Dickens Howzat?

Andersen Ah, yes, yes, Dicken – the cricket. Oh, oh, I am – athlete with no hope. Bear. Goose.

Catherine He must have his Prince Albert pudding before he plays cricket.

Dickens In earlier years, Andersen, Catherine was the finest female silly mid-on in England.

Catherine Is that a compliment?

Dickens It is intended as such. (*Gathering himself.*) Pudding before cricket for you, Andersen. (*Agitated.*) I find it hard to sit tonight. Forgive me, Georgina, I must go out instanter. Send out the boys when you have puddinged them up.

Catherine You won't wait?

Georgie He cannot wait, Catherine.

Dickens (*going*) I cannot. I cannot.

Walter Cannot we go with him, Aunt Georgie?

Plorn I want to play cricket.

Georgie I think you might, just this evening.

Catherine Georgina, it will be better for their stomachs if they wait.

Georgie If Charles can do some violent action with the cricket bat, he will be assuaged a little. He is so shocked by Jerrold's death.

Catherine He was also my friend when I was young.

Georgie Of course, Catherine, I understand.

Catherine You do not understand. Or rather, I do not understand. I do not understand.

Georgie Walt, take your little brother. He can go out also. It is beautifully warm and pleasant.

Kate Is there any chance I might steal Plorn for an hour? It is so much easier to draw from life.

Catherine What did you say, Kate?

Kate I really did not say anything, Mama. I was thinking out loud, and not very fascinating thoughts. Ignore me.

Georgie (*to Walter*) Go, go.

Walter Yes, Aunt. Well – (*Ceremoniously.*) Well, Mr Andersen, we would be most awfully blessed and happy to have your company outside.

Andersen What, what?

Catherine Good boy, Walt, but let Mr Andersen stay here. (*To Andersen.*) The poor child – he is practising to be a grown man. But he is not, Georgie, he is not.

Georgie Run away out, Walt, with Plorn, and raise the rooks in the beech trees.

Walter We will, Aunt. We will bombard them like Russians.

Walt kisses his mother.

Catherine Dear Walter.

Walter (*a moment*) If you'd rather I stayed here with you, Mama, I could easily forgo cricket. I am also very fond of Prince Albert pudding. It is a speciality of Mama's, Mr Andersen. Did you know Mama has written a lovely cooking book?

Catherine starts to cry.

Georgie Away out, away out.

Walter (*dismayed*) Yes, Aunt.

Plorn Don't forget me, Walt.

Walter Silly mid-off for you, Plorn.

Catherine (*to Andersen*) My poor Walt is to go to India in a very few days. A country heaving with rebellion. He is being sent out to learn to be a soldier.

Andersen Oh?

Georgie It will set him up in life.

The sounds of cricket off.

Catherine It is like going to the edge of the known world in an old story. I do love the boy so much. I fear it may kill me to see him go.

Dickens (*appearing*) Bring us out tea when you come, ladies. It will be something to wash that terrible cold soup out of my mouth.

Catherine Cold soup in France tastes different than in England. Why ever so, I could not say.

Georgie Hush, the soup was perfect soup.

Andersen (*holding his stomach, to Catherine*) I think, dear lady, stomach – surge. I must go to my place where sleep . . .

Catherine Poor, poor Andersen. You see, Georgie, it was not good soup.

Andersen stumbles into the dark guest room and takes the chamber pot desperately and, on the other side of the bed, hurriedly unhitches his trousers.

Andersen Oh, oh, oh, oh, oh, oh.

Andersen groaning and shivering, the sound of Dickens and the children playing at their cricket, the light failing in the branches of the beech trees, the boys laughing and calling, Dickens energetically playing, shouting, instructing. The sound of the piano, playing Mendelssohn.
Now Dickens visible, bowling to his unseen son.

Dickens Oh, that's a poor ball. I have lost that swing in my arm. I must practise when I am alone, and then startle you all with my improvement.

Aggie comes out with the tea. Walter comes on holding a bat.

Walter Oh, that's wonderful, Aggie.

Dickens Good girl, Aggie, good girl. You are a treasure. (*Drinking.*) You look peaky, Aggie. I will send you to Dr Bill.

Aggie I'm all right, sir.

Dickens The Irish make perfect tea.

As Walt takes a cup from Aggie, he touches the back of her hand a moment.

Aggie They don't *make* tea in Ireland, sir.

Dickens No, only little maids. When we are fortified, boys, let us play on, while the light remains to us. Thank you, Aggie. You have taken the cold out of us. If Franklin and his men had had this tea in their icy world at the frozen North, boys, there would have been no death and dying. Thank you, girls, for the wonderful music. Thank you, boys, for your wonderful batting and catching.

Light now on Andersen. His face frightened and unhappy.

Andersen Little maid? A girl should not see an old man in travail. How I fear this sadness. God look down on me, and send me a day of simplicity and ease.

Light fading from Andersen. Voices from another room. Andersen listening.
Catherine sitting in her bed in her nightcap and gown.
Catherine is reading a little book of poems. Dickens has a measuring stick and is measuring.

Catherine What are you doing, Charles?

Dickens I am measuring.

Catherine What are you measuring?

Dickens The distance – between two points.

Catherine And why, Charles?

Dickens Because – I – it will be easier perhaps to block the door to my dressing room.

Catherine It is very convenient for you, going in and out that way.

Dickens It was. But now, I find I wish it to be inconvenient – and inaccessible, except from the corridor outside.

Catherine But that is not an improvement.

Dickens No. In architectural terms. But yes, in – sentimental terms.

Catherine I do not understand you.

Dickens I do not think I understand myself. Indeed, I am like a man on fire – like a sailor in a plunging ship. Like a fierce, buzzing fly without its wings.

Catherine It's time to sleep. I can read no more of these *Four Seasons*. It used to calm me. I have reached the end of Spring and I am exhausted. I will blow out the candle, if you do not mind.

Dickens And leave me in the dark?

Catherine I will obviously wait till you are in bed.

Dickens staring at her.

What?

Dickens I am fixed to the floor. I wonder if it is not a symptom of madness to be unable to rest, even when quite still? Two foot six and a half inches. I will just note it down for the carpenter. I will go and do so. I won't wake you, never fear. I will creep back later.

Catherine What is the matter?

Dickens There is nothing the matter, in the proper understanding of the phrase.

Catherine If you say not.

Dickens I say – go to sleep. Go to sleep. Go to sleep.

Catherine I will not sleep easily, with Walter going away.

Dickens We should be thankful there is a great Empire to mop up these sons.

Catherine To mop them up? These boys I love? That you love. Are the rest to follow? Will you send Plorn also at close of day?

Dickens I am hoping, I confess, that Plorn may manifest some talent that will keep him in England.

Catherine But because Walter is a nice, simple boy, and not your favourite, he must be thrown to the wolves of Empire?

Dickens The Empire does not disdain those lacking a particular talent. England does. I have tried to place Walter everywhere. I have failed because he can do nothing, in particular. It was Georgie suggested India. I think she is right.

Catherine Georgie. They are my sons, they are my sons.

Dickens Well, well, come now, Catherine, let's not pretend you had the doing of them. It has been Georgie mostly has tended them.

Catherine Not at my request.

Dickens The house must have order.

Catherine Now you are getting angry.

Dickens I am not getting angry.

Catherine If Georgie has helped me, it is because I have crawled from childbirth to childbirth. She of course has not had to do such things. Is that indelicate of me to say so? And little Dora, my own angel . . . What was I to do about that? That horrible place I had to go to afterwards, and that loathsome sadness.

Dickens Malvern, so horrible? It is a very nice place where you took the waters. So the living make fools of themselves with little things. And speaking of foolishness – Andersen. He was trying to tell me he needed to go to London to see his friend, the Danish ambassador Count Reventlow. You see how easily it can be said? It was like listening to the *Iliad* in a Hottentot translation. To cap it all, I had just read a horrible notice of *Little Dorrit*, so I listened to him *through my tears*.

Catherine (*laughing suddenly*) Poor Charles.

Dickens You laugh at me. You are right. (*A moment.*) Do you think, Catherine, he is quite real? Perhaps only a ghost? It suddenly seems strange to have him in the house. A haunting. To have anyone in the house. To stand here myself, with you. To be a living person. It is all strange to me, suddenly. The house standing in the darkness, the marshes darkened, the blue of the Thames darkened to pitch, only the stars brightening, as if for fear of the dark's victory, and in these bedrooms, the inhabitants sleeping, dreaming – dreaming.

Catherine And we should do the same.

Dickens (*moving away*) Poor Douglas, poor Douglas . . . He had five little babes that he loved so much. Now they have no father.

In the corridor outside he encounters Kate.

Kate Papa, are you unwell?

Dickens No, Kate dear, I am not unwell.

Kate You are very pale, Papa.

Dickens It is the moonlight.

Kate There is no moon tonight.

Dickens There is a moon. What is that, if not a moon? You are not very observant.

Kate But that is not why you are so pale, Papa, you are not the man in the moon, you are the man on the earth.

Dickens Yes.

Kate Where are you going now, at this moment?

Dickens I am going to my workroom, to make a note of something. Two feet, six inches and a half.

Kate Oh? What does that measure? Will I go with you?

Dickens Will you come with me? I would like that, Kate. I am glad we are friends again.

Kate When were we not?

Dickens When Charlie Collins wrote to you last month, and asked you to marry him.

Kate Yes, and for a moment I thought I might like to, and then I thought I would not.

Dickens Even though he is Wilkie's brother, how could I countenance anyone taking you away from me? You have written to the poor man, to let him know your answer?

Kate No, but I will do so.

Dickens Everyone is in their beds?

Kate Walter said he might go and try for sea trout. Otherwise, all are in their beds.

Dickens embraces Kate.
Darkness falls equally on everything.
Walter returning through the dark garden with a fishing rod and a brace of trout. He goes into the house.
Music. A few moments.

Cockcrow.
The sun flooding the garden and house like a wave.
The sea in the distance, sparkling, new.
Aggie comes in to Andersen.

Andersen Ah, little maid.

Aggie Yes, sir?

Andersen I wake.

Aggie Yes, sir.

Andersen You did never take my clothes last night and flatten them?

Aggie Flatten them, sir?

Andersen Make them flat for the morning.

Aggie No, sir, I did not think to press your clothes, that is true, sir.

Andersen And my linenings, privy linenings, not gathered from the chair. (*Putting on his gown.*)

Aggie No, sir. I wouldn't dream of touching your private things, sir, without your say so. Besides, my hands were not clean. I had been gutting Mr Walter's fish.

Andersen In houses of princes they are washing my linenings. I also require to be shave.

Aggie What?

Andersen Shave, shave?

Aggie Well, sir, I know nothing about that.

Walter passing outside.

Master Walter, do you know anything about shaving? My guess is, no.

Andersen Could this boy be ask to shave me, little maid?

Aggie Do you mistake the poor boy for a servant, sir?

Andersen Oh.

Walter (*angrily*) The nearest barber is in Rochester, Mr Andersen, and that is a fair journey by the horse and carriage. (*To Aggie.*) Was he suggesting *I* shave him, Aggie? What an idiot he is.

Andersen I am by the minute growing to animal with pins in body.

Walter He should not ask me to shave him, Aggie, and if he does again, I will likely do so, and slit his throat while I do, like Sweeney Todd.

Aggie Don't be such a goose, Master Walter. The man barely knows what he is saying.

Walter Don't you call me a goose.

Aggie Oh, and I will, and worse too.

Georgie comes by.

Walter Here's Aunt Georgie. I suppose he will ask *her* now.

Georgie Ask me what? Poor Mr Andersen, we are crowding in his doorway, and he is quite *déshabillé*. Excuse us our fantastical rudeness. They are such narrow halls here.

Andersen Shave me!

Georgie What? (*To Aggie.*) You may give him one of Walter's sea trout for breakfast.

Aggie Yes, ma'am. Weren't he so clever to catch them?

Walter They throw themselves on the hooks this time of year. What I love best of all is the darkness.

Georgie There was a bright moon the whole night.

Walter Not under the trees there by the river. It is lovely there.

Andersen May I call carriage, Mrs Georgie?

Georgie Oh?

Andersen To go to Roch-es-ter.

Georgie To Rochester? Why ever so?

Andersen For barber.

Georgie But, my dear Andersen, Mr Dickens and Charlie will take the carriage now to Higham station. I'm afraid you will be marooned here till it returns. We all will be, temporarily.

Andersen When I make command, you must do. This is law of hostility.

Georgie You mean hospitality, sir. Good gracious, sir. How is it, sir, that a person who exhibits such wonderful fine feeling in his books, can exhibit such a wonderful bearish aspect in his person?

Andersen What, what? You say what?

Catherine arrives.

Georgie I am not about to translate my own anger, sir. That would be quite absurd.

Catherine Georgina, you will not insult our guest.

Georgie I do not insult him, Catherine, he does not speak English.

Catherine I speak English, I hear you. You will not distress Mr Andersen.

Georgie This is quite insane.

Catherine Ah yes, ah yes?

Georgie This is not rational.

Andersen Madness. Madness.

Dickens arriving.

Dickens What is this? What is this phantasmagoria of distress? (*To Andersen.*) You are weeping, sir? Who is not weeping? I demand to know who is not weeping, so I can confer on them the much admired, much desired Order of the Dry Eye.

Georgie It is this person causes this mayhem, Charles.

Dickens May there not be quiet in my house? May there not be peace in my kingdom?

Georgie (*going*) A bizarre, intolerable, crude person . . .

Catherine You must admonish her severely, Charles.

Georgie goes.

Dickens I must go to London. Charlie, Charlie, come down, we must go, we must go.

Charlie Yes, Papa.

Dickens Andersen, adieu.

Dispersal. Catherine on her own.
 Clock striking in the house, the hum of sunlight.

Georgie (*furious, coming back to Catherine*) I do not know why you are so obvious in your unhappiness, Catherine, I really do not.

Catherine Excuse me, sister?

Georgie I counsel you to find peace in yourself.

Catherine You wish to be in charge of me also? You wish to be in charge of my children and my household and also of me?

Georgie I merely wish to create tranquillity and general pleasantness, so Charles can work.

Catherine Nothing, no force known to man or God, could prevent Charles from working.

Georgie I think you thought once that I was necessary and useful.

Catherine After all these latter births, you were useful, you were in every way a wonder. But Plorn is nearly six, and I am more robust, and my spirits are good now,

37

better by the day. We are here in this new house. My ambition is to be happy here. You must not become atrocious to me. (*A moment.*) Wait, wait, wait, wait.

Catherine holds Georgie's arms, puts her head down.

Let us not be at war, let us not be at war, the two of us . . .

They embrace. Georgie goes.

Time passing.
    Catherine, alone now, in the sitting room by the fire. Outside, finches and other small birds singing. Aggie comes in to her with her bucket.

Aggie Do you want me to keep the fire going, Mrs Dickens? It is very sunny.

Catherine Do, do, please, Aggie – how this cold creeps in about my legs.

Aggie I am always cold, ma'am. That's what comes of eating only a little, and carrying coals and scantlings all the day.

Catherine I hope you will not say we don't feed you, Aggie. I rather think you have fattened out of late.

Aggie I won't fit my pinnies in a bit.

Catherine Just keep the fire going, Aggie, and do it – discreetly. That is how things are done in a good household.

Aggie Yes, Mrs Dickens.

    Aggie goes out into the garden to dump the cinders. When she reaches the door, Kate is just coming in. Kate stops out of sight when she hears her mother speak.

Catherine (*to herself*) It is not as if anything terrible has occurred, beyond harsh words, beyond being accused of lethargy. I accuse myself also of fatness, of a certain disgustingness of form brought on by bearing so many children year after year. Oh, when little Dora died, I so wished to grieve, but *his* grief was so much greater, so much more *important* – and something of him went down with her into the underworld, leaving me with half a ghost, half a shining man.

Walter appears in the garden.
Walter and Aggie snatch a kiss, checking they are unseen.
Catherine crying.

I make no sense, I make no sense. When we should be quiet, after the day, he becomes agitated, wakeful, watching me closely, till I am thinking he is noting every wobble in my poor body, and remembering years ago, when it was often said I was like a wraith, a beautiful ghost. I always got compliments when I was a girl, far more than Georgie. He said I was the loveliest creature he had ever seen. And wrote me such letters.

Kate bustles in. Kisses her mother.
There's a strange sound from somewhere.

Catherine (*after a moment*) What is that wailing sound? Do you hear a wailing?

Kate (*listening*) I do. (*Looking out.*) It is Mr Andersen, Mama, down by the roses.

Catherine What is he doing?

Kate Wailing, Mama.

Catherine I should go and join him, and we can wail together.

Kate takes out a letter from her pocket. She just holds it.

39

Time passes, the whirr of darkness, the clocks in the house sounding.

It is night again, Walter crosses the garden as before with his rod.
    Andersen is walking in the garden. Walter doesn't see him in the dark.

Andersen Young sir.

Walter My God, Andersen, my heart nearly leapt from my chest.

Andersen Excuse. But I am grateful for moment to say, sorry for bad moment this morning.

Walter Which one, Mr Andersen? Do you refer to your suggesting that I shave you?

Andersen Yes. Most stupid, young sir.

Walter I am Walter Dickens, a son surplus to requirements, sir, you do not need to apologise to me. It was no surprise to me that you thought me a servant.

Andersen You are teasing, sir.

Walter As the son of a great man, I have met all the great writers of the age. Thackeray, Tennyson, Longfellow and poor Jerrold. I am sure I should be flattered to be apologised to by the greatest living writer for children.

Andersen For children?

Walter Perhaps it sounds odd in Danish.

Andersen It sound odd in all language. But I only wish to say my sorry.

    Andersen holds him by the arm. There is something of a proposition in the gesture.

Walter (*taking his arm away*) That is quite all right.

Andersen Remember, young man, all souls are equal. It is the law of God.

Walter I am sure you are mistaken, sir.

He is crying.

Andersen You are weeping? You are sad.

Walter I am not weeping because I am sad. There are varieties of weeping, sir. I am weeping because I am alive. And it is extremely odd to be talking like this out in the garden.

Walter moves on past.

Andersen Did you catch fish?

Walter One cannot catch fish every night.

Andersen Our Lord Christ, only He always catch fish? (*More fluently.*) Are you a believer, sir? Of course. I have seen the gold and jewels of a thousand churches, all over the world. My God is my redeemer and my hope.

Walter Sir, you have lost me. I do not speak that language. I presume it is your own native Danish?

Andersen Ah, I slip, I slip – sorrow, sorrow.

Walter goes.

Now the distant music of Handel's Messiah.
    A sense of the soaring pillars of the Crystal Palace, fountains, glass, light.
    Catherine and Andersen sit side by side, the thousands of voices singing, the music pouring against them. Their faces look out, rapt. In a strange light, an indistinct figure brings a lighted candle. Light burns around her.

41

Catherine Oh, Mr Andersen. It is a young girl, with a single candle, for innocence, I expect. How beautiful it is.

Andersen Beauty, beauty, beauty.

Change of light, vanished palace, Dickens' sitting room again.
Catherine and Andersen in the same position, but in the seats by the fire. Aggie – the innocent girl – is putting a taper to it.

Catherine Aggie, you did not keep the fire going for us while we were at the Crystal Palace.

Aggie I did, ma'am, but it went out.

Catherine Firelight, it is rather kind and good, do you not think, Mr Andersen?

Andersen Often I sit in my room in Copenhagen with fire, and outside, outside the window, there is the harbour so familiar, the little light of the sea, and I am for the moments, in that time, Mrs Dicken, happy. All terrible things pass away. When I was a young boy, you see, Mrs Dicken, I feared so many matters. And I still fear.

Catherine Yes, you see, that is what I think also. That is what I think.

Aggie sweeping the hearth of ashes, blowing the fire into flames again.

Andersen Then we are in the same thought.

Catherine Your English is becoming good, Mr Andersen, because your mind is always thinking so clearly behind the words.

Andersen Thank you, Mrs Dickens.

Catherine Aggie, are you finished there?

Aggie Yes, ma'am – just.

Andersen She is – the Ash Girl – among the ashes. The Ash Girl becomes princess, little maid, at end of story. Not all stories end so happy.

Aggie A princess, sir? I don't think so, sir, begging your pardon.

Andersen I applaud your honesty, little maid.

Aggie You give me the *bualadh bos*, sir.

Andersen What is that?

Aggie It is Irish, sir, for applauding.

Andersen *Bualadh bos.* (*Clapping his hands.*) Now I speak English *and* Irish.

Catherine I will go up in a minute and give Plorn a kiss, although I suppose he will be asleep. I hope so.

Andersen I have no child to kiss.

Catherine But I suppose you have thousands, the thousands that read your stories?

Andersen Well, well. Yes, yes. But none to kiss at night.

Catherine No. (*A moment.*) Your mother is not living, Mr Andersen?

Andersen No, madam.

Catherine You were very close, I am sure.

Andersen Yes, yes. But very – poor.

Catherine Oh?

Andersen Yes.

Catherine You weren't born in a princely house?

Andersen Ah, ah.

43

Catherine You have all the qualities of a prince. Charles also had difficulties when he was a child. He never speaks of it, but it is always there. Sometimes I see that child in his face. You have not married, Mr Andersen?

Andersen No, no, I have never marry. I have loved, please do not think I have not. And I am old, but still I hope . . . I am the bachelor of the old comic plays, no? Never marry, but I have been able to observe that difficult – landscape.

Catherine Yes. What excellent English, again, Mr Andersen. It is so good to talk. I know you have trouble understanding me. Perhaps that is a mercy.

Andersen perhaps does not understand, but he lays a hand on Catherine's arm.

Andersen Dear lady.

The sound of Dickens returning.

Catherine (*brightening*) Ah, here he is. Back from the city.

Andersen (*jumping up*) Ah, ah.

Dickens comes in.

Dickens You are cosy in here. (*Humorously.*) Mr and Mrs Andersen.

Andersen Dear Dickens. Welcome.

Catherine How did your arrangements go, Charles?

Dickens That was long since. I got down from the train at Rochester. I have walked the remainder of the way. I have stamped along the roads, hour after hour, tireless, feeling more energy, *more* energy rise into me, mile by mile, intolerable. But I have established a place and a time for our rehearsals for *The Frozen Deep*, and devilish difficult it was. In the old days, it was easier.

Catherine (*fervently*) Wonderful old days.

Dickens Perhaps. Yes, one longs for that. When everything was to do, and our limbs fair. And no idea, not a notion, that it could ever come to this. Not an iota of an intimation. I long, I long for that. Do I reject the present? I reject it, I revolt against it. Intolerable. A sort of torment, all the more horrible for being commonly endured. I would go back. Wind back the clocks, I order it. (*A moment.*) You were certainly a most wonderfully adept actress in that time. Yes. That is true, that is true. And beautiful. That is true, that is true.

Catherine It is the doing of things properly that is so important. To have a great talent as you both do, what a mercy. That I might paint like Kate – I do pray she continues to do so, fiercely, savagely. I think I must look in my heart, in this latter part of my life, and find what it is I can *do*. That is the grace of life.

Andersen Yes, yes.

Dickens (*a moment*) And so –

Dickens looks like he is going to go again.

Catherine (*rising*) I will come with you.

Dickens Well, well, if you say so. Good night then, Andersen.

Andersen walks up to him and kisses him.

Andersen Be assure – great love, gratitude.

Dickens Of course, Andersen.

Catherine and Dickens outside the room now, downstage.

I did not wish to embarrass you in front of Andersen, but I fancy I will sleep in my dressing room tonight.

Catherine Oh, Charles, that won't be comfortable for you.

Dickens Did the carpenter come by any chance to block the door?

Catherine No, he did not.

Dickens Ah, you see. If I ran my magazine on such casual grounds it would not last a month. You see, you see, I am exhausted. Myself and Wilkie did a reading of the play, and I am so very tired. And have not slept well these last weeks.

Catherine But the play is written, no, Charles? And you have performed it before? So beautifully.

Dickens Thank you, Catherine. Yes. But it stirs up the mind. You remember how fantastically demanding the role of Wardour was. That final scene, where I die. Even as I ran the lines, in a casual manner almost, I looked up, and I was astonished to see Wilkie was weeping, that hard young man that never weeps.

Catherine It might be better if he wept for the real world, and not a mere play. I hear such scandalous things about Wilkie these times. I wonder should we even have him here at the house any more? A man that keeps an establishment of two women in odd circumstances is not company for my two daughters.

Dickens That is all nonsense. He is a fiery man, that is all.

Catherine You are angry again. I cannot bear this anger.

Dickens God's eyes, I am not angry. Let him be happy in his life, odd as it may be. He is my friend. He is advising me. (*A moment; then, too vigorously.*) Don't you see that that play is as real as real life? More real, more clear?

46

Catherine I love you, Charles.

Dickens What did you say?

Catherine says nothing.

I did not hear you. It doesn't matter. Let us not discuss it.

Catherine What is Wilkie's advice to you?

Dickens It was in confidence. To be told to no one.

Catherine Even to me?

Dickens Is there a licence in marriage to break the confidence of a friend? No. There is a licence, of course, to chain one wretched beast to another. (*A moment.*) Excuse me, Catherine. Unhappiness makes me rougher than I would like. He said that something would happen, and that when it did, I would know what to do. There would be clarity. (*A moment.*) I will make up my bed in the dressing room.

Catherine I thought for a moment when you praised the person I was of old that you were praising me in the present. I deluded myself. What joy there was in that delusion.

Catherine goes. Aggie emerges, gives Dickens a candle. Andersen listening.

Aggie Good night, sir.

Dickens (*sighing*) Aggie. Now, now, tell me, tell me plain – is what Dr Bill tells me true?

Aggie hangs her head.

Aggie Don't, sir. Please.

Dickens Now, child. There is obviously a boy involved?

Aggie I suppose so, sir.

Dickens Evidently, unless you have emulated a certain young woman of Nazareth. Is it someone nearby?

Aggie says nothing.

Well? (*No answer. Then, angrily despite himself.*) Well, it either is or it isn't. Oh, why do I have these misfortunes brought down on my head? (*A moment.*) Not Charlie, I do hope and trust? Not any of mine? Not Walter – he is only sixteen.

Aggie (*terrorised, weeping*) No, sir. No, sir, no one at all. It was a different boy, sir, a different boy. Oh, God help me.

Dickens How could you do this when you have such a good situation?

Aggie And I am happy here, sir.

Dickens How could you imperil all? Oh, I have seen this a thousand times. Why am I surprised? A 'follower', Aggie, would have required an immense – certification from your mistress. (*A moment.*) Will this lad stand by you?

Aggie No, sir, because we parted.

Dickens Then he is a scoundrel as well as a –

Aggie Or I should say, he was parted from me, by fate, sir.

Dickens Oh? And who is he, this fateful person?

Aggie He was – a young soldier, who got – a medal at Sebastopol, sir. A Victoria medal, sir, just like what you said at dinner. Which was the why it made me gasp, sir. To hear you say it, and it all an accident that you were saying it. And then he went to – Madagascar, two months since. And, and he was killed by a cannon shot, in the adventure of the war, I am told, sir.

48

Dickens Is that a story, Aggie?

Aggie No, sir.

Dickens That was a brave boy.

Aggie He was a brave child, yes, sir.

Dickens It is extraordinary. You have suffered. You lost both your good parents in the Irish hunger, I know. You are suffering now. (*A few moments.*) But I think you must prepare yourself to leave us, Agnes. Of course you must. You know that. I will try to make arrangements, of course.

Aggie I am so happy here, sir.

Her terrified face, weeping.
  She goes.
  Now Kate again, her face inserted into the light.

Kate I was looking for you, Papa. (*After a moment.*) Papa, why you are causing so much unhappiness to Mama?

Dickens Ah, well now, that is a matter for the parties involved.

Kate You are becoming almost brutal with her.

Dickens (*shocked*) What? Brutal?

Kate If you do not mend your ways, I shall never be kind to you again.

Dickens I believe you, Kate. How you flare up, little Lucifer.

Kate We are happy in this house. I am happy here. It is paradise.

Dickens Everyone is happy here, it is a great nuisance.

He holds her arms, shakes them gently.

Be my daughter. Be more like your sister Mamie, gentle and true. Do not torment me.

Kate I do not wish to be *authored* by you.

He starts to move away.

You are bringing away the light, Papa.

Dickens Then follow after me, child.

Darkness, music.
    The marsh owl.
    Light on Kate's easel, with a half-finished portrait of Plorn in his Sunday hat, with the black ribbon.
    The sound of the marsh owl's wings.
    Catherine stooping over the sleeping form of Plorn, to kiss him.

Catherine Good night, little boy. In your beautiful sleep. The guest of darkness is in the garden. The roses are tightly sleeping.

Dickens standing, singing 'Oft in the Stilly Night'.
    A sort of storm of colour, dark greys and browns, blows against him. Music.
    Darkness, music.
    The marsh owl calling like a strange morse signal.

Act Two

Some days later. At a mirror, Catherine passing, actively trying not to look in it, a glance, pat of the stomach, then passing on much discomfited, then . . .

Aggie, Kate and Georgie are standing in a row, facing out, with a table before them with bowls of flour, jug of milk, rolling pins, bowl of meat etc. They wear white aprons. Kate sings 'The Minstrel Boy', taken up by Aggie. They are working now all the while, kneading pastry, rolling it out, egging it, putting in the meat, moulding it, trimming, sticking on lids etc.

Dickens and Andersen in chairs as if in a different room, drinking tea together.

Aggie I never thought I would see ladies making pork pies. If you live long enough you will see everything.

Georgie I think it is particularly right for women to work. And I despise a woman that knows nothing about it.

Kate Suppose the world were to come to an end, what would we eat at the End of Days, if we couldn't make things for ourselves?

Aggie Well, miss, you mightn't have pigs then, so you mightn't have pork pies.

Georgie That is very true, Aggie.

Kate goes to the door.

Kate Mama, Mama, come and make pork pies with us!

Dickens You hear that? Caterwauling, and in a gentleman's house.

Andersen laughing.

Georgie I don't think she will come.

Kate I think she will come.

Working again.

And, Aggie, where were you before us, that you never saw ladies working?

Aggie Big place in London, miss. I was only eleven when I came there, straight from Ireland. Lady Wicklow's house, ma'am. I didn't know a pile of linen from a hayfield, miss.

Georgie laughs. They work on.

Georgie I do not know what we would look like to an outside eye.

Kate I tell you, Mr Charles Collins would be happy to paint us. He would be happy to paint you, Aggie. He would call it 'The Little Maid' or 'The Innocent'.

Aggie Innocent, miss?

Georgie Or, 'The Eve of St Agnes'. (*Laughter.*)

Kate He is a lovely painter.

Aggie Who, miss?

Kate Mr Collins. He has been down here, Aggie, you have met him – he is the brother of Mr Wilkie Collins.

Georgie Well. (*A moment.*) You have a big day looming, Kate. Your father all in a fluster, all in a knot. The Queen coming to a private showing of *The Frozen Deep*, *he* won't meet her, because he will have all his make-up on still after the little comedy he will do with Wilkie Collins after, and he wrote to her equerry and said he could not appear to Her Majesty *in character*, and it takes him forty minutes *to find his face again*.

Aggie The Queen. Oh, miss. I would love to see the Queen.

Kate It is terrifying.

Georgie But it is wonderful also.

Catherine appears, putting on an apron.

Kate Mama. There now, Aunt, I knew she would come.

Catherine Did she doubt me?

Catherine sets to.

Georgie Speaking of linen and beds, Aggie, you watch Mrs Dickens now, there is no one on earth who can fold a pork pie like Catherine Dickens.

Catherine Nonsense.

Laughing. She certainly can beat out the pastry. They all work away.

Where is Plorn? He usually haunts the kitchens.

Kate When he saw me coming, he ran for it, dreading I was going to ask him to sit for me again. How he detests sitting still.

Georgie That is the first duty of a six-year-old boy, never to sit still.

Catherine Indeed. I was wanting to congratulate him on making friends with Mr Andersen. The first time he saw him, and Mr Dickens introduced them, Plorn said, 'But he is a horrible, horrible man, Papa, throw him out the door.' 'Before we give him tea?' says Papa. (*Laughter.*)

Aggie Janey!

Catherine (*laughing*) Luckily, I don't think Mr Andersen understood the word 'horrible'. At any rate, just this morning I saw them, Mr Andersen doing those wonderful cut-outs for him, Plorn's face transfixed, windmills, clowns and Lord knows what else, those elegant long fingers working with the scissors, very wonderful, very. And just then Papa comes in, and Plorn looks up at him, innocent as a foal, and cries, 'Oh Papa, let us throw him *in* the door.' (*Laughter.*)

Aggie Throw him *in* the door . . . That's very droll, ma'am.

Kate Oh, Mama, you are the funniest woman alive. You are.

Georgie Throw him *in* the door. The dote. Fancy. Little fellow of six.

> *They work on. Soon they have a pork pie in front of each of them. Catherine's is adjudged the neatest and the best. Much laughter. The scene fading.*

Dickens Well, great laughter, great laughter. But we are peaceful here.

Andersen Great peace, Dicken.

Dickens What fascinates me, Andersen, about the tradition of folk tales in Denmark, in Germany, is the sense that they come from the oldest places, the darkest places. And yet are subtle, and true, like your own stories.

Andersen I thank you, dear Dicken.

Dickens Yes. And the appetite everywhere for such depictions. The brothers Grimm. And the like.

Andersen Ah, I meet brothers Grimm. Two time. First time, they pay me no heed. 'He is nobody,' they say in silent. Second time, I have made books, I am the famous man in all Europe, they say, 'Hello, hello, Andersen.'

Dickens (*laughter*) Well, you are the most famous writer on earth now. You eclipse me. I should take umbrage. I should object.

Andersen Oh Dicken, Dicken . . .

Dickens You are a great sun, and little suns like myself must struggle to show our light.

Andersen But I am not great. Small, small. Every word of censure hurt me. Newspaper. Torture.

Dickens (*rising to leave*) Andersen, I bid you henceforth live by my own precept, which I follow religiously or try to. That is, a man should read nothing in the newspapers that he has not written himself.

Andersen laughing. Dickens laughing. Dickens goes. Andersen alone, blatantly happy.

Andersen (*doing Dickens*) 'What fascinate me of tradition folk tale Denmark . . .' 'I thank you, dear Dicken . . .' (*Laughing.*) Such friendship. What joy, what joy.

Then this clearing, and . . .

Some days later again, Dickens with a cane, and Andersen, walking together, Georgie and Walter following, carrying rackets, Aggie carrying a basket, Catherine with parasol. Kate with her easel. They are walking up Telegraph Hill. Kate catches up to Walter.

Kate Walt, I envy you going away. What an adventure. All that way to go and all those sights to see.

Walter Well, I am glad you envy me. But I would rather stay.

Kate You're young, it's good to venture out into the great world.

Walter Then you go out into it.

Kate Ah, but I am a woman. They have things arranged quite differently for us, you know. I set out on my adventures inwardly, into my pictures. I think you have it better than Charlie, helping Papa in cold, dank London.

Walter I would love to help Papa. I would love it. I would be near the things I love.

Kate And you will help Papa, by going, Walt.

Walter Is that what he said?

Kate No, or not the way you think it.

They move on, then:

Dickens Yesterday I endured the black tedium of a London funeral. Now, we are climbing this hill. The sun is shining, the birds are singing.

Dickens glances at Catherine, who is going along sadly. He turns his head away.

I have never climbed this hill before, and I do so now, on your recommendation, Andersen. Henceforth, let it be known as Andersen's Hill.

Andersen (*looking about*) Paradise, paradise.

Dickens Ah yes, ah yes.

Walter with Aggie.

Walter Can I carry that for you?

Aggie You cannot carry it.

Walter I went up to your door last night, you would not answer my whistle.

Aggie You need to stop mooning over me, Master Walter.

Walter I am not mooning over you. I am going away soon.

56

Aggie And why are you going away, do you even know why?

Walter I am going away to help my father.

Aggie Help your father. You leave me be now and don't be coming whistling at my door. Creeping into the garrets at night, and you are lucky your Aunt Georgina hasn't spied you yet. How can you think to invade my little room, when it is the only place I have to myself in the house?

Walter I want to kiss you, Aggie.

Aggie Oh, kissing, now. I've had enough of kissing, thank you.

Walter Are there pork pies in the basket, Aggie, do you know?

Aggie Of course I know. I packed it, you goose. We women made them.

Walter Young cousin Hogarth went out last year to India, Aggie, to the very same place I am going, and he is dead now. I go out to fill a dead man's shoes.

Aggie That makes no blessed odds to me. I am an Irish girl. The land of the dead. My mam and daddy died in a ditch, and four brothers and sisters were thrun in after. I survived all that, only to be tormented by you.

Now Andersen and Dickens. Kate briefly with her father.

Kate Please go to Mama, Papa, she is very disturbed, and I cannot find the words to comfort her.

Dickens I will go to her in a moment.

Kate Then you do feel it too?

Dickens What, Kate? What am I to feel?

Kate You are disturbed also? Mama is disturbed, I am disturbed, and you are disturbed. (*A moment.*) What is the matter with everyone? What is amiss with everyone?

Dickens Kate. We are having a picnic at the top of this hill – that is the theory, though this hill appears to have no top.

Kate moves away.

Andersen And, dear Dicken, this play, this *Frozing Deep*? What is?

Dickens *The Frozen Deep*. What is, indeed. I wrote it with – no, I am lying already, Wilkie wrote it, and I pushed it about, for certain purposes of my own, having an evil intent by it.

Andersen Evil?

Dickens To make the audience cry! Do you remember, Andersen, that scandalous story about Franklin at the Pole, that his men had been forced by extremity to cannibalise each other? It was a tale told to a newspaperman of poor ability by an Esquimaux. I have written extensively on this calumny. An Esquimaux. A savage, sir, worse than an Irishman. My friend Carlisle has written, if the Irish cannot be improved a little, perhaps they ought to be exterminated. He might have spoken of the Esquimaux.

Andersen (*trying hard to follow*) Hmm, hmm?

Dickens We can imagine an Esquimaux, at the edge of the frozen lands, telling such lies to whomsoever might ask – with the meat of Franklin's men in his belly. Of course. Guilty. For someone ate those men. The gnawed bones were found. Teeth marks, Andersen . . . But I say it was not Englishmen that did such a deed. There is something noble and essential in the English character, in the English soul, that cannot drop to such depths. Even forced into the very pit of suffering, like my character Wardour, something at last rises up, and forbids dark conduct, and so such a man is redeemed by his – Englishness.

Andersen Englishness? (*Distressed at not quite understanding – but nearly.*)

Dickens Was there ever a landscape as beautiful as this? How I wish I could have shown Jerrold this beauty.

> *Catherine hurries to catch up and holds Charles by the arm, panting.*

Andersen, will you ever so kindly?

> *Andersen understands and moves away a little.*

Catherine I am quite out of breath.

Dickens I am exhausted, trying to make myself understood to Andersen. His English comes and goes, like a little season all of itself. Catherine, you must steady yourself.

Catherine I am not to be steadied with a word.

Dickens I did not sleep in that little room last night. I went out and walked under the pine trees like a ghost. Then over the dark earth to Higham, like a homeless soul, the trees breathing along the white road, and rounded the sleeping village with my dogs, and came back – none the wiser, none the calmer. There was an owl that called the whole night over the marshes.

Catherine I heard it too.

Dickens It was like an echoing phrase, but what it was saying I cannot tell.

Catherine It is saying perhaps, *love your wife.*

Dickens Catherine, Catherine.

Catherine I love you still, Charles. I will always love you.

Dickens Catherine, Catherine, Kate and Georgie are just there, and Walter, and poor Andersen, he frightens so easily, let us not burden them with our difficulties.

Catherine What is it that offends you, what is it?

Dickens Nothing, nothing, I do not know. If I had the words to tell you, I would tell you.

Catherine I have no one to turn to for advice.

Dickens Look, look, I believe that is the summit. At last.

He pulls away from her. She is left bewildered.

Catherine (*to herself*) I will always love you. But who is this 'I'? I, Catherine Dickens? I feel as if I have left my body, and am looking down on myself. Give mercy to me, dear Christ, give mercy.

Georgie comes back to her.

Georgie Are you all right, Catherine? You seem much distressed.

Catherine I am much distressed. I do not just seem it.

Georgie We can enjoy the pleasant sunlight, can we not, as of old?

Catherine Georgie, it is not as of old. In all honesty you have done something to me that is so grievous I cannot find a phrase for it in English, or any other language. Is it true that you thought it a good thing that Walter would go away?

Georgie If only to answer the awful struggle of his father to find a place for him in the world.

Catherine Georgie, I must be plain and clear. There is something deeply amiss. I will write to Mama and ask her might she not take you back. I do not want to uproot you, I am so so grateful to you, and I love you, but we cannot go on like this, or I will die.

Georgie I am so unhappy to hear you say this. I would not hurt you, Catherine, I would not.

Catherine (*touching her arm*) But you are hurting me, Georgie. And I can see that it is I who must make it stop.

The summit.
   In the distance there is the crump of artillery shells.

Andersen What is that, Dickens?

Dickens It is the guns of the Earl of Ulster's Regiment, practising in the hills.

Walter Ah, ah, Sebastopol.

Dickens Yes, yes. (*He is moved.*) Poor Jerrold.

Andersen lays a hand on Dickens' shoulder a moment.
   Music.
   Walter again with Aggie.

Walter Aggie, Aggie – I need to say – I love you.

Aggie You love me? (*After a moment, fiercely.*) I am in the family way, do you know what that is?

Walter Oh, I . . . (*He opens and closes his mouth.*)

Aggie (*imitating him*) 'Oh, I . . .' You look like a dying trout. You're only a baby yourself. (*Contemptuously.*) You needn't be worrying, Master Dickens. I will see to myself. *I* am not an *amadán*.

The sound of the crickets in the grass, the burning sunlight. Walter thinking hard.

Walter (*very genuinely*) I do not think you understand me, Aggie, when I say I love you. If I am old enough to be a soldier in India, then I am old enough for you to believe me. I will – I will find a cottage for us, at, at Broadstairs, yes, by the sea, where we used to play as children, and you and I will live there, with, with the baby.

Aggie And what will you feed us with, and what will you clothe us with? And will we be having a marriage, in the church in Rochester, and will that be a Catholic marriage, pray, good sir, or an English one? And will your people sit on one side, and mine on the other, if I had any? Maybe the bishop would like to marry us?

Walter I will – I have seen the Broadstairs folk there picking winkles when the tide is out. I am sure I can pick winkles. (*Realising that sounds absurd.*) Or some kind of work.

Aggie stares at him a moment, shaking her head, and moving away.
Dickens walks away a little apart now with Georgie. Kate and Walter are playing at shuttlecock. Aggie busied with the picnic things. Andersen watching, applauding, trying to be helpful.

Dickens I want to rush out on the landscape with my dogs, and forge ahead alone, faster and faster, to make this strange turmoil drop from me.

Georgie These are troubled times.

Dickens She is my mirror and I have the urge to smash it in pieces.

Georgie Who is your mirror?

Dickens Your sister. Her face is my mirror, I peer in there and see my face.

Georgie How do you mean, to smash it, Charles?

Dickens If it means choosing between myself and your own sister, I will understand if you must side with her. You have been her helpmeet, after all, these many years.

Georgie (*fearfully*) What do you intend, Charles?

Dickens I hardly know. You have been mother *de facto* to the children. Of course, it is evident, she has grown madder these last years. It began in those exhausting days when Dora was born, and then when the little one died . . .

Georgie I know, I know. But what are you going to do?

Dickens Wilkie, he has been advising me, of course. He knows these subtle matters. What a perfect friend he is. (*A moment.*) I want to suggest to her that she lives here while I am in London, and in London while I am here.

Georgie Oh, Charles. Are you not fearful of the response of all those who love you?

Dickens Fearful? It is all fear. But I am in the right. They will see that. If they truly love me, they will see that. (*A moment.*) When there are dinners, of course she must preside, to present a united face to the world.

Georgie I think that would be a terrifying thought for her. I must be honest in my response to you. I do not think you should send her away. That would be a disaster for us all. (*A moment.*) And you will want to send me away also?

Dickens Never, Georgie, never. Unless you wish to go?

Georgie (*a moment*) Whatever happens, I will wish to stay at your side, and do my work as always, the children, and the house.

Dickens But do you understand, Georgie, the depth of that wish? Would it not in all truth serve your own life better if you were to find a loving husband? I cannot obviously offer myself in that role. This is a thought that nearly drives *me* to madness. Do you understand?

Georgie There are many forms of living. I would gladly, in every sense, give myself to you.

Dickens In English law, that would be given a very black character, I am afraid.

Georgie I am quite capable of loving you without that aspect.

Dickens Do you truly say that?

Georgie I do. There are many forms of love not scorned by God.

Dickens Then I will believe it. I need you now, I will not deny it. If Catherine has grown mad, I am also nearly mad. My head aches as if struck and struck again with hammers.

Dickens grips her hands.

But you relieve me of a profound disquiet. Thank you, thank you.

Georgie I am ever in your service, Charles. Indeed, to be separated from you and the beautiful light that shines around you would be like a death to me.

Dickens Faithful, faithful girl.

There is a moment when he might kiss her. Andersen boisterously laughing.

Georgie Charles, when is Andersen to leave us?

Dickens Oh, that is an even greater mystery. His letter said two weeks, but it is now, two, three? To test him out the other day I asked him to stay for the opening performance of *The Frozen Deep*, thinking he would graciously decline and reveal his departure date. But he graciously extended his stay instead.

Andersen looking his way innocently, smiling.

Georgie He was due home yesterday, and arrived very late, in tears, with these extraordinary bulges in his stockings. He had been in Rochester, and had hired a jarvey to bring him back, and it took a road he did not know, so he assumed the jarveyman was going to bring him to a quiet spot and rob and murder him.

Aggie, apart from everyone, sitting stooped on the ground, distressed and quietly crying.

So he put everything into his stockings, his moneybook, his diary, any books he had, for their safety I presume. The poor jarveyman, a perfectly respectable example of his trade, said his passenger began to scream, just beyond Higham.

Andersen observing Aggie.

Dickens He has the habit of kissing me on the lips, which is frightful. Surely there should be a law against that. He is a most profound, original and wonderful artist, but a spectacular nuisance of a man. He loves being here, and I grow a little fearful that he may stay for ever.

Andersen approaching.

Like another child – an elderly, lunatic child. He has nothing else to do, besides visit the ghastly princes of Europe in their crumbling castles. It is no wonder to me that no woman has ever attached herself to him.

Georgie Charles, Charles.

Now Andersen reaches him, smiling.

Andersen (*scanning Dickens' face*) You are perfect well, Dicken?

Dickens Dear Andersen. I am well.

Andersen You look tired, Dicken.

Georgie (*to Andersen, sharply*) It is customary in England, sir, to make no reference to a person's state of well-being.

Andersen Excuse, madam? How strange. (*Nearly touching Dickens.*) Your eyes, sir?

Dickens My eyes?

Andersen There is – ghost in eyes.

Dickens Andersen, that is upsetting. What do you see?

Andersen (*very sincerely*) Young girl in rags, bent by wind.

Dickens I have no ghost in my eyes. When I was a little boy, Andersen, and the days of my life seemed bleak, I ordered things about me as if I were the stage manager of my own fate, and improved everything by conferring upon it the lie of romance. But no ghosts.

Andersen Dicken, I also child sit in ruin of life, and make play.

Dickens We were brothers then, and did not know. We have come up this hill, let us go down it. We have money to gather for a widow and her babes, in the real world of England below, which is a mighty serious business.

Walter comes up with Kate.

Catherine (*at a distance, hopelessly*) Charles, Charles.

Kate Papa, what is going on? Remember what I said to you.

Dickens Yes, yes.

Kate I will hate you, Papa, bit by bit.

Walter Mama is on her own.

Georgie She is not on her own, she is with us all.

*While the house and rest are re-established by light,
Dickens in the garden. Catherine reaches him.*

Dickens My dear, this is what used to be termed a
spectacle.

Catherine I am quite composed. (*Fixing her hair with
effort.*) It is the sultry air and the walk has affected me. I
am quite myself, and full of plans. Charles, I am resolved
on a transformation. I intend henceforth to be forthright,
active, living.

Dickens That is admirable, of course.

Catherine In furtherance of this plan, and believe me for
the greater good of yourself, myself, and the children,
I wish sincerely to ask if Georgina might not be sent back
to our mother Mrs Hogarth, having done most wonderful
service to me, to us . . .

Dickens says nothing.

Dickens I cannot in all conscience just at present see the
purpose or good in that, Catherine. But, I will think on it.

Catherine You will think on it?

Dickens I will.

Catherine Thank you. Most obliged to you, Charles.
I am most obliged – and happy. And I will always revere
what she has done for us here. Always. I do thank you,
Charles.

She goes.
Walter comes to him.

Walter Father –

Dickens Now I think I get the speech where you remark upon your great unwillingness to leave us, and the great injustice of my sending you out so far.

Walter No, Father, it is not that matter. It is another matter.

Dickens That is a little phrase which a parent does not like to hear.

Walter It is Aggie, sir.

Dickens Aggie, sir?

Walter She is, I do not know the proper word for it, is it *enceinte*?

Dickens *Enceinte*?

Walter Yes, sir, and it is my fault, and I wish to ask your permission to take a little cottage in Broadstairs, perhaps, and to take up employment there, that will support her. When I am put up against necessity, I am sure I will meet the challenge.

Dickens What? (*A moment.*) You fool. All my sons are fools.

Walter I am very fond of her, Father. I love her.

Dickens You are not the father, Walter. I have already spoken to Aggie. She was very clear about it.

Walter That is not true, sir. There is no one else. She has told you something that you have chosen to believe. If you believe it, you choose to believe a fiction.

Dickens (*great anger*) I do not, sir. Allow me to be an expert in that department.

Walter is close to weeping.

You have let yourself down. You are in disgrace with yourself and your God. We will not speak of this again. You will go to India.

Dickens walks away from him.
Walter goes off disconsolate.

A few moments without light, then slowly a tableau downstage. Theatrical light. Andersen sits watching 'the play'.

Andersen (*to himself, correcting his English*) The Frozen Deep, The Frozen Deep . . .

Dickens lies on the ground as Wardour with a webbing of rags over his clothes. Kate in character as Wardour's lost love kneels to him, weeping. Dickens is giving his last speech but there is no sound. Catherine comes on, but dressed as Queen Victoria. Andersen bows to her, she sits, watches. Then the last sentences of the play become audible:

Dickens . . . Nearer, Clara – I want to look my last at you. My sister, Clara! – Kiss me, sister, kiss me before I die!

Then Kate lowers her face to the face of her father; he has died. After a moment, the weeping Queen begins to applaud. A weeping Andersen follows in the applause.

Queen Such a beautiful illustration of the English character.

Andersen (*to the Queen*) Bualadh bos, bualadh bos.

Queen What do you say, sir, what do you say?

Andersen It is Irish, Majesty. Applause, applause.

Queen Ah, the Irish, sir. The Irish.

All suddenly dispersed.
  Andersen alone, downstage now in his shadows.

Andersen Gods of England, protect me. Queen of this England, pray for me. Let not the great expanse of Dickens quite occlude me, let there be a niche of fame for me, so then I can love him with a free heart. And as I fear God's opinion, so I fear Dickens, and his rejection of me. I pray, I pray. And may God forgive me for my terrible vanity.

Andersen away.

Some days later. Dickens pacing in the garden.
  Kate comes out to him, holding the page of a letter.
  She hands it to him. He reads it. Looks at her.

Dickens This is a different letter to the letter we discussed. In this letter you intimate you will accept Charles Collins. This is not part of my friendship with Wilkie. You cannot accept him without my permission.

Kate You will give it.

Dickens How will I give it? Am I to see my daughter dressed in a wedding dress, an item just the same to me as a foul outfit of mourning, and to take all her beauty and life and wonder out of my house?

Kate Yes.

Dickens I know for a certainty he has no money.

Kate I will make my way as a painter. And if I fail in that, I will go on the stage.

Dickens You will find the professional stage a great change from our pleasant little enterprises. The theatre is full of people so terrible they will make your hair stand on end.

Kate Then I will go about so – (*She plucks up her hair.*)

Dickens What causes this change?

Kate All that you are, all that you have done, all that you are going to do.

> *Kate takes her letter and goes.*
> *The sound of the Thomas Moore song played somewhere in the house on the piano.*

The sitting room of the house. Catherine, and Kate coming in with the letter, weeping. Andersen overhearing.

Catherine Kate. Will I ring for some tea?

Kate No, Mama, no tea. Oh, forgive me. I am a ninny. But the tears will not stop.

Catherine Dear Kate – I am sorry you are so distressed. Sit down, my dearest, sit down and tell me what has upset you.

Kate Oh, I cannot, Mama. (*Suddenly.*) I was leaving for Higham in the carriage yesterday. Something stopped me, Mama, something made me want to return. I turned the carriage back in a strange desperation and rushed into the house, flew through the hall, feeling that I would never see him again if I did not fly, fly, and stood in the door. I watched him as you might a person in a dream, not certain that I could truly reach him, or ever make him hear me. He was bent over his work as always, writing in that same dark ink, line after line, like a voyage. After a long moment he turned, but said not a word. I ran to him. He opened his arms, like a father, and caught me in his arms, and embraced me, and kissed me.

She breaks down even further.

Catherine Oh, Kate. But, he *is* your father.

Kate Oh, Mama, Mama, what is wrong with me? I do not weep like this except when I play that stupid part in Wilkie's play, as Papa's lost love.

Catherine Kate. You are wonderful in that, and not at all stupid.

Kate It is terrible to see Wardour die. It is terrible to see Papa die. My papa.

Catherine It is like a true bereavement. It wrenches the heart.

Kate Now. I will dry my tears. I must be sensible.

Catherine He just does not understand how everyone and everything depends on him.

Kate Who? Papa?

Catherine Yes. Kate, let me just say, let me just say, in truth and simplicity, I love you. My daughter. Everyone here loves you.

Kate (*laughing*) Even Andersen?

Catherine In particular Andersen. He is not so strange as others make out. He is a fine and feeling man.

Andersen's face hearing this.

What are you going to do, dear?

Kate I am going to begin my life. Something is ending, and so I will begin.

Dickens comes in.

Dickens Begin what, Kate?

But Kate starts to go out. As she passes the finished portrait of Plorn, she throws a cloth over it. Then, in the shadows as the scene progresses, she takes off her dress as if in her room, drapes it over a chair, and exits.

How one loves one's daughters. It is quite extraordinary.

Catherine She is a wonderful girl.

Dickens She is a marvel.

Light only on the chair where Kate's dress is. Dickens goes to the dress, kneels to it, holds it to himself and weeps.

Dickens It is because of me – but how is that, how is that? Oh that I were a better father – a better person.

Then back with Catherine.

Why did I come in to you? Aggie. She has managed to – you understand? The usual matter with young girls. It is a great pity.

Catherine The poor child. Child is all she is. It will be in itself a desolating experience, God knows, and to lose her place on top of that.

Dickens Of course, she must go. She cannot stay here.

Catherine No, no, of course she cannot.

Dickens I am trying to help her. I am – *putting my mind to it*. Hush now, hush . . .

Georgie enters now with Aggie, leading Miss Ternan, a small pretty woman, about eighteen.

Well, she comes, early.

Georgie Charles, may I introduce Miss Ellen Ternan? She has an appointment I am assured.

Ellen divesting herself of a nice coat and bonnet, giving the items to Aggie.

Dickens She does. Most certainly. (*Going to her.*) Thank you so much for coming all this way.

Ellen It is a wonder to me to meet the author of all my favourite and most loved books. Am I impossibly early? I am so sorry. I can wait, Mr Dickens. Just put me somewhere out of the way and I will be quiet as a mouse.

Dickens Not at all, you will have luncheon with us, by my eyes. By your accent, I surmise – Yorkshire?

Ellen Irish by birth, sir. I was in Yorkshire a good while as a child.

Dickens Ah, Irish, the Irish, a noble race, a race of renown in the theatrical arts, Boucicault, yes?

Ellen My father and mother both worked for Mr Boucicault. On one occasion she played Gertrude to Macready's Hamlet. I am told Macready is your great friend?

Dickens Wilkie Collins chooses wisely. That is wonderful. I am sure you will do very well. You will be required to do a great many things in your role, but chiefly, to weep. I hope you are a good weeper?

Ellen I hope so. I hope your daughter Kate will not be angry with me?

Dickens Why would she be angry, my dear?

Ellen For taking her role?

Dickens She cannot play it in a big theatre. She has not the voice for it.

Dickens holds her by the shoulders quite fiercely.

She weeps with genius, I will allow. Every night, when we play it, the whole house in a sort of stupor of grief, her tears pour down upon me, soaking my beard, her little face a moon above my own, as I die upon the ground. To die in such a way gives me a strange feeling afterwards, like freedom. I cannot explain it. It rests me, miraculously.

He pulls her to him a little with a strange energy. Ellen pulls away slightly. A moment. Then Andersen clears his throat.

And this is Mr Andersen, the great Danish author.

Andersen smiling benignly.

Ellen I have not advanced very far into Danish literature, forgive me.

Andersen's face.

Andersen Most melancholy to hear.

Ellen (*to Dickens*) I have just finished *Little Dorrit*, sir, and it is the most deeply affecting book I have ever read.

Andersen Oh, oh . . .

Dickens Charming. Let me introduce you to my wife, Catherine.

Catherine You are very welcome here. The people of the theatre are welcome in this house.

Ellen (*to Catherine*) My mother sends her best regards and asks that you forgive her for sending me without a chaperone – she intended to do that task herself, but has been snagged up in town.

Dickens Snagged up', how charming. We will look after you. Kent is horribly staid and safe.

Catherine Please thank your mother for her regards.

Dickens When you came in, I thought there was a trick of light, and that a white fire from the hall followed you in. Like a little ghost. Such a lovely, sincere face.

Ellen I am moved by your words.

Andersen I am poet, poet of Denmark.

Dickens Let us go in and eat. We will refresh you after your long journey. And I think you must say something nice to Mr Andersen later. I will school you up on his stories. You will be an expert on Danish literature by the time I have finished with you.

Ellen laughing. Her laughter brings Catherine's gaze.
   Music. They go off together, Dickens deep in talk with Miss Ternan.

Catherine alone, like a portrait, looking out on the view, a music as if moving against her. Walter comes to her in his East India cadet uniform. She brushes the lapels slowly, smooths his hair, face nearly expressionless.

Walter Mama, if before I went I had something to tell you, something that might be considered in some light as – as shameful?

Catherine My child, you are not capable of a shameful act. You are sixteen.

Walter Boys go to be midshipmen at fourteen, Mama, and they are accounted men.

They embrace. A darkening picture.

Then noise of trains, steam.
   The shadows of great ironworks rising to the skies.

Dickens and Walter, in his cadet uniform, stand opposite each other. Andersen near them, but at a respectful distance.

In the shadows, Catherine in the sitting room beyond. Georgie comes in and comforts her.

Dickens I am sending you out, Walter, to a fine and dutiful life in Bengal.

Walter Yes, Papa.

Dickens And thinking of you as a little boy, and that you are the first to go. (*A moment.*) We must not be unmanned by the task of saying goodbye.

Andersen (*to himself*) These are eternal sorrows.

Dickens Your going so far away is naturally distressing.

Walter Yes, Papa.

Dickens Soon your heart will lighten, and your road will seem to stretch out in front of you brightly, and you will be glad to be on it.

Walter Yes, Papa.

Dickens Goodbye, my son.

An embrace, a moment, then Walter turns to go.
Before he is quite gone, he turns and salutes, and goes.

You see, Andersen, what distress you saved yourself by going about the world on your own.

Andersen Dear Dickens, dear, dear Dickens.

Dickens goes forcefully to Catherine. Andersen looking thoughtfully after him.

Dickens Catherine, you must be brave.

Catherine I will never be brave again.

Dickens There is always sorrow in the management of children. Childhood closes like an iron door, it cannot be opened again.

Catherine Call him back, Charles, call him back – why do we need to send our child so far?

Dickens Catherine, Catherine, poor Andersen will be affrighted. The whole house will be affrighted. Georgie . . .

Georgie brings salts to Catherine.

Catherine You defeat me. I am like one of those old cities in the Bible. One city builded upon another. You are building your own city on top of me.

Georgie Because you have dragged a boulder onto your own breast, and it is crushing you, does not license you to say that I put it there.

Catherine Oh, Charles, I pray you, send her away, send her away.

Dickens Enough of sending away, enough.

Dickens appears to be going, but he does not go. He says nothing for a few moments. Then suddenly:

And I do think in all honesty this is the time to communicate to you my decision *vis-à-vis* our future arrangements.

Catherine What, Charles?

Dickens Wilkie could explain it better, were he here. It is a very good, simple plan. You will live in London and I will live here.

Catherine This is your plan, that you made with Wilkie? But how could such a plan be made, and your love for me be still included? Such a plan does not include love.

Dickens It may be, in the natural way of these things, that such a thing as love may be discounted here. A person, in order convincingly to live, must breathe, and I cannot breathe.

Catherine In my company, you cannot breathe? I could not agree to such a plan. The boys will be home soon from school and I must be thinking about that. There is so much to do.

Dickens There will be no need for that. You will not see them, Catherine. You will not see any of them, do you understand? My mind is quite made up.

Catherine Could God kill me now, do you think He might, of His great mercy?

She looks to Georgie, but there is no help there.

Dickens You are to be happy, on your own terms, in your own house.

Catherine And quite alone.

Dickens I have written to your family's attorney, we have conducted ourselves with perfect propriety, and you are to be provided for, and you are to be free in so far as you are a married woman living apart from her husband.

Catherine If you had devised a series of tortures for me, if you had hanged me in Tyburn and drawn out my entrails, wherewith I made my children, you could not hurt me more.

Georgie and Dickens disperse.

Catherine alone.
Dickens encounters Aggie in the garden.

Dickens I have made arrangements for you, Aggie, you will be happy to hear. My friend, Miss Angela Burdett-Coutts, and I have set up a house called Urania Cottage, as a refuge for fallen women. You will go there, and when all is done, we will find a place for your baby, and I will arrange for you to go on to Canada, so you may start again afresh.

Aggie (*after a moment*) I will not go to the place you mention, sir.

Dickens Oh?

Aggie I am not a fallen woman. I am an Irish girl of sixteen years and I will go back to Ireland, sir, and see what my people can do for me.

Dickens That is brave, Aggie, of course. But if they cannot do anything? The world will be against you.

Aggie I will do something for myself, and damn the world, if you will excuse me saying so, Mr Dickens.

Dickens I think you may be excused the word. I think you may be justified in choosing it.

Aggie goes on to Andersen, packing in his bedroom. Sunlight sparkling everywhere.

Aggie The weather has picked up at last, sir. And is it very far to go, Denmark, sir? Here is your rope, sir, you must not forget that.

Andersen It is far. It is journey of – transformation. Train, carriage, ship, walking, new looking, great noises, England falls away, this hard language, and then I am at home, and speaking Danish again.

Aggie I think you like it, sir, that travelling?

Andersen Ah, maybe so, little maid.

Aggie I like it too. Well, sir, be sure and have your pocket handkerchiefs handy to yourself when you need them. Just in case, sir. I have washed and folded them.

Andersen Thank you, thank you.

Aggie I hope you will not forget Gad's Hill, sir?

Andersen Memory everything. Thank you, little maid. Thank you for drying my eye when first I come.

Aggie Oh, sir, yes, I remember. It does seem a long, long time ago.

Andersen (*handing her a note of money*) Yes. I have been here long time. Too long for Dicken, too short for me.
Aggie (*the money*) That is a great sum of money, sir.

Andersen I, what is word, surmise, you will need it.

Aggie Oh.

Andersen I am not blind in the eyes. I cannot say English, but I see, I see. (*Differently.*) But not everything. I think there is trouble somewhere, but what trouble I do not know.

Aggie Every family has trouble, sir, it comes from trouble, and goes to trouble, and just maybe is trouble, sir, plain and simple.

Andersen You are wise, little maid.

Aggie Not so much. Safe journey to your home place.

Andersen God bless and keep you.

Andersen goes in to Catherine in the sitting room.

Andersen Dear, dear lady. Thank you, thank you.

Catherine (*with great effort*) My dear Mr Andersen, so sorry to see you go, infinitely sorry.

Andersen kisses her hand.

Andersen Ah, yes. I wish you all happiness, in your life, Mrs Dickens, and in your perfect and holy marriage.

Catherine Now, truly, your English is perfected.

Andersen I thank you.

Dickens and Andersen at the dock.
Noise of ship, passengers, ordinary turmoil.

Dickens You have everything you need?

Andersen Oh, sir, the love I have for you. *By my eyes.*

Dickens My dear man. My dear man.

Andersen steps up to Dickens and kisses him on the
mouth. Dickens quite still.
The ship calls to the passengers.

It is time to go up the gangway. Here is a little book. I
wrote in it for you?

Andersen goes off, speechless, waving, Dickens
waving.

Goodbye, Andersen. (*Then quietly.*) Goodbye, Andersen.

Then Gad's Hill again, Catherine seated, and Georgie,
Dickens returns into the scene.

Well, although we may say we suffered a great deal from
Andersen, the poor man is gone.

Georgie You are certain, Charles? You saw him on to the
ship?

Dickens He kissed me, we parted.

Catherine stays severely alone, her face in pain. Aggie
comes in with kindling etc.

Catherine (*with effort*) He was a good, kind, dear man.

Georgie He was a terrible old bore, that is the truth.

Catherine What will happen to us now?

Dickens Only splendid things.

Aggie Will I light the fire now, ma'am?

Dickens No need, Aggie.

Aggie goes.

I do believe the month is quickening at last, and we will
have the proper summer soon. I will sit out in the garden
with my book, and Mamie will sit near me, quietly
talking. We will be English folk in England – the happiest
people on earth in the happiest country.

*Music, and the scene acquires the aspect of a genre
painting. The faces picked out by light. A moment.
    Then Aggie, in her coat and carrying her scant
possessions, comes out of the house, goes to the edge
of the stage, stops there, looks back.
    Light now on Aggie.*

Aggie I used the money that kind Mr Andersen gave me
to go back to Ireland. My people were all dead, but I got
work in a kip in Monto, to serve all the soldiers that were
in barracks there in Marlborough Street, in the city of
Dublin. When my son Walt was born I went on with that
work, until he joined the army himself and went off to
India with the Dublin Fusiliers and did well at the little
wars there. Then he came home and didn't he bring me
on then with him to America, and fought in the last wars
there against the poor redmen. And then we crossed up
into Canada, myself and him and his wife. And I died an
old old woman in Calgary, Alberta.

She goes.

Music.
    Now it's twelve years later again, Andersen in his room in Copenhagen, talking to Stefan, the clink and knock of boats in the harbour below.
    The figures of the others still visible behind.

Andersen And that is how all stories end. Soon Mrs Dickens was ejected, for no fault of her own, exiled from all she knew and loved.

Stefan And is the poor woman still living, Andersen?

Andersen She is, I believe. Her grief will be very great, for I tell you, Stefan, by every word of her mind and gesture of her body, it was so clear she loved him. Perhaps great genius must always be tied by the heel to unhappiness. I have often thought that. The world delights in us, we delight in ourselves not at all.

Stefan My dear Andersen.

    Light on Catherine.

Catherine I lived for twenty years in the house in Gloucester Crescent that Charles provided for me. My son Charlie chose to live with me, but for many years I saw none of the other children. My beloved Walter was dead within five years, not of the wars and rebellions that he so feared, but an aneurism in his poor head. He lies in some lonely graveyard in India. All my sons were sent out into the world, Plorn the last at sixteen, away out to Australia, never to come home. I never saw Charles again. Kate married Wilkie's brother, and was widowed young. Of course I could not attend the wedding, nor could she come to me. Then, some years after Charles died, Georgie came to see me. She gripped my hands and asked for my forgiveness. I gave it. I begged her to be sure that Charles's letters to me as a young woman would go to the British Museum, so that the whole nation would know that he loved me once.

Light on Georgie.

Georgie I stayed, and minded the house with Mamie and all the children. I weathered as best I might the foul intimations of that dark aftertime, namely that Charles had preferred my own person to my sister's. Even that I was the true mother of the children. At Charles's request I was examined by the doctor, and found to be *virgo intacta*. Eventually that wretched storm subsided. I did what I could to understand Miss Ternan. Nothing was ever truly the same again.

Ellen Ternan comes on and stands in the shadows near to Dickens.

When Charles died I edited his letters and looked after his sacred legacy. I was the dog with saucers for eyes guarding the treasure, like in the Andersen story. I lived to be an old woman, into a century I did not understand. But I understood Charles, heart and soul.

Andersen What is the world but a great empire of sadnesses? (*The newspaper.*) Here is another. No more stories will flow from him.

Stefan By your own grace of mind, you might have counselled him.

Andersen My dear child. I wore myself out trying to show myself to him, and perhaps wore him out also.

Stefan And yet you speak so well of him.

Andersen Stefan, you see, I loved him. My reverence for him has been unaltered by the stray bits of news that have reached me here these last years. Poor Dickens. Did he take comfort from his little actress? I do hope so. Have his daughters and sons forgiven him? But you see, but you see, dear Stefan, I include all that and still the sum comes out the same. I loved him.

Stefan holds his arm.
Light on Ellen.

Ellen If I may say – if I may be allowed to speak – yes, I loved him, though I shrank from his touch. In the twelve years of our love he aged into an old old man. He was only fifty-eight. He fell ill in our little house in London. I brought him in the carriage to Gad's Hill. I had promised Georgina I would not let him die in my house. When we got there, he asked to be put on the ground. His daughter Kate held him in her arms just a few sad moments and he died. Then, I mourned a while, and married a schoolmaster in Margate and never breathed a word about that strange, fled life.

As one, Catherine, Ellen and Georgie slowly raise their hands and put them over their faces.

Andersen When I was leaving on the last day I could barely speak, I kissed him, and we parted. All the way to Gravesend he had brought me, and as the ship steamed out of the harbour, I looked back, certainly not expecting to see him, and there he was, on the last rough stones of the pier, standing in his bright yellow waistcoat, waving his hat in farewell, faithfully, faithfully waving.

Dickens steps forward, raising his hat with a slow flourish.

Dickens himself. Great friendship, like a conflagration, cooling to silence.

Stefan kisses Andersen on the mouth.
More light on Dickens. He sings 'The Last Rose of Summer', the company join in, then a last flourish of his hat, raised high, banishing everything.